Quick Guide

ATTICS

CREATIVE HOMEOWNER PRESS®

Editorial Director: David Schiff
Author: Mark Feirer
Copy Editor: Kimberly Catanzarite
Associate Editor: Alexander I. Samuelson
Art Director: Annie Jeon
Graphic Designers: Michelle D. Marchand
                   Karen Ellis Phillips
Illustrators: Ray Skibinski, Paul M. Schumm

Cover Design: Warren Ramezzana
Cover Illustrations: Paul M. Schumm

Electronic Prepress: TBC Color Imaging, Inc.
Printed at: Quebecor Printing Inc.

Current Printing (last digit)
10 9 8 7 6 5 4 3 2 1

Quick Guide: Attics
LC: 94-069652
ISBN: 1-880029-42-1(paper)

CREATIVE HOMEOWNER PRESS®
A Division of Federal Marketing Corp.
24 Park Way
Upper Saddle River, NJ 07458

C O N T E N T S

SAFETY FIRST

Though all the designs and methods in this book have been tested for safety, it is not possible to overstate the importance of using the safest construction methods possible. What follows are reminders; some do's and don'ts of basic carpentry. They are not substitutes for your own common sense.

■ *Always* use caution, care, and good judgment when following the procedures described in this book.

■ *Always* be sure that the electrical setup is safe; be sure that no circuit is overloaded, and that all power tools and electrical outlets are properly grounded. Do not use power tools in wet locations.

■ *Always* read container labels on paints, solvents, and other products; provide ventilation, and observe all other warnings.

■ *Always* read the tool manufacturer's instructions for using a tool, especially the warnings.

■ *Always* use holders or pushers to work pieces shorter than 3 inches on a table saw or jointer. Avoid working short pieces if you can.

■ *Always* remove the key from any drill chuck (portable or press) before starting the drill.

■ *Always* pay deliberate attention to how a tool works so that you can avoid being injured.

■ *Always* know the limitations of your tools. Do not try to force them to do what they were not designed to do.

■ *Always* make sure that any adjustment is locked before proceeding. For example, always check the rip fence on a table saw or the bevel adjustment on a portable saw before starting to work.

■ *Always* clamp small pieces firmly to a bench or other work surfaces when sawing or drilling.

■ *Always* wear the appropriate rubber or work gloves when handling chemicals, heavy construction or when sanding.

■ *Always* wear a disposable mask when working with odors, dusts or mists. Use a special respirator when working with toxic substances.

■ *Always* wear eye protection, especially when using power tools or striking metal on metal or concrete; a chip can fly off, for example, when chiseling concrete.

■ *Always* be aware that there is never time for your body's reflexes to save you from injury from a power tool in a dangerous situation; everything happens too fast. Be *alert!*

■ *Always* keep your hands away from the business ends of blades, cutters and bits.

■ *Always* hold a portable circular saw with both hands so that you will know where your hands are.

■ *Always* use a drill with an auxiliary handle to control the torque when large size bits are used.

■ *Always* check your local building codes when planning new construction. The codes are intended to protect public safety and should be observed to the letter.

■ *Never* work with power tools when you are tired or under the influence of alcohol or drugs.

■ *Never* cut very small pieces of wood or pipe. Whenever possible, cut small pieces off larger pieces.

■ *Never* change a blade or a bit unless the power cord is unplugged. Do not depend on the switch being off; you might accidentally hit it.

■ *Never* work in insufficient lighting.

■ *Never* work while wearing loose clothing, hanging hair, open cuffs, or jewelry.

■ *Never* work with dull tools. Have them sharpened, or learn how to sharpen them yourself.

■ *Never* use a power tool on a work piece that is not firmly supported or clamped.

■ *Never* saw a work piece that spans a large distance between horses without close support on either side of the kerf; the piece can bend, closing the kerf and jamming the blade, causing saw kickback.

■ *Never* support a work piece with your leg or other part of your body when sawing.

■ *Never* carry sharp or pointed tools, such as utility knives, awls, or chisels in your pocket. If you want to carry tools, use a special-purpose tool belt with leather pockets and holders.

SIZING UP THE PROJECT

The cardinal rule of remodeling is to size up the situation before spending any money. First take a close look at the attic to determine what can be done with it. Then learn enough about building codes to keep your project on the right course. It is harder to correct mistakes than it is to avoid them in the first place.

Checking for Trusses. If this is what you see inside your attic, forget about an attic conversion. Trusses should not be removed or altered.

Investigating the Attic. Lay boards over the tops of exposed joists before spending time in the attic. Secure the boards temporarily so they do not shift as you walk on them.

Nails

Surveying the Attic

Once you decide to convert an attic to living space, you must determine whether or not the job is possible. Not every attic can be converted to living space, and some of those that can be converted are not worth converting. To find out more about the possibilities for your attic, head up there with a tape measure and flashlight.

Checking for Trusses

A roof that was built using trusses, rather than individual rafters, cannot be converted. If the attic is filled with diagonal framing members, called webs, it was built with trusses. Webs give each truss its strength and cannot be removed without causing the trusses to fail. If the trusses fail, the entire roof has to be rebuilt. If this is the situation with your roof, but you still need more space, your best solution is to convert the basement (if you have one) instead.

Investigating the Attic

If the roof is supported by standard rafters, there may be enough room to convert the attic to living space. However, before you can know for sure, you must investigate further. Temporarily nail some 1x4 or 1x6

boards (or plywood if there is enough room to get it up there) across the tops of the attic floor joists. This prevents you from accidentally stepping through the ceiling. It provides a much safer platform from which to work. Never step directly on insulation; it almost always is supported by drywall alone and cannot support your weight.

Headroom. According to code, there has to be enough headroom in an attic conversion to enable you to move about comfortably and safely without clobbering your forehead every time you turn around. To get an idea of whether or not your attic is even close to meeting this standard, take a quick measurement between the ridge and the top of a floor joist. If it does not show at least 7 feet 7½ inches (1½ inches accounts for the thickness of a finished ceiling and floor), you cannot convert the attic without major work and a variance from local building officials.

The complicating factor in figuring attic headroom is that the ceiling slopes. Because of this, some of the floor area is worthless for use as walking space even though it may be perfectly suitable as storage or working space. Recognizing this, the building code calculates headroom

requirements in the following way: To begin with, all living space in the attic must be at least 70 square feet in size, and measure no less than 7 feet in every horizontal direction. A very small room, or one that is long and narrow, is not considered suitable living space. In addition, at least 50 percent of the floor space must have at least 7 feet 6 inches of headroom (the rest can have as little as 5 feet). Finally, portions of the room with less than 5 feet of headroom are not considered living space, so you should not count them in the calculations above.

If the roof framing has collar ties, take headroom measurements from the floor to the underside of the ties. Also, if the flooring does not exist yet, subtract 1½ inches from each measurement you make to account for the thickness of floor and ceiling finishes.

Ventilation. During the warm seasons, an attic becomes the hottest area of the house. This problem must be addressed before turning the attic into a living space. Proper ventilation through the roof spaces, as well as through the room itself, is crucial for comfort even if you plan to air-condition the space. By addressing the ventilation possibilities now, you can determine whether or not converting the attic is worth the trouble.

You need at least one window on each end of the attic to encourage an adequate flow of air. You may wish to add at least one dormer window or a ventilating skylight to improve ventilation, even if the dormer is not needed to improve headroom. If a chimney at one end of the attic prevents you from installing a window there, a dormer or skylight nearby can provide the necessary air circulation.

Measure the depth of the existing rafters to see if there is enough room for fiberglass insulation plus a 2-inch air space above the insulation. The air space ensures that moisture migrating into the insulation is carried away. It also helps to keep the roof assembly cool in warm weather by providing a ventilation path immediately beneath the roof sheathing (see page 74). The ideal ventilation pattern draws in the air through soffit vents and exhausts it through a ridge vent. However, any combination of vents placed low and high encourages air movement.

Rafters. Rafters that sag noticeably may be dangerously undersized. Sags may be the result of too many layers of roofing, or improperly sized rafters. To determine the severity of the sag, stretch a string along the bottom edge of one rafter and measure the amount of sag at the midpoint of the string. If rafters sag more than 1/2 inch, you may have to install a structural knee wall to support them (see page 72).

Caution: *It is imperative that this work is done properly, however, so consult a structural engineer before proceeding.*

If only one or two rafters sag, check them for cracks, open knotholes or other damage. It usually is easier to repair damage than to replace the rafter. Straighten the rafter (if possible) and bolt new wood over the damage (much as you would splint a broken arm). Sometimes a 2x4 can

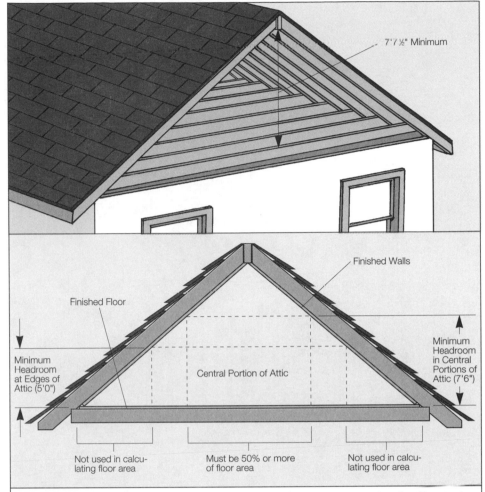

Headroom. If the distance between the ridge (or the underside of collar ties) is not at least 7 ft. 7½ in. (top), your attic probably doesn't meet code requirements for a living space. The diagram (bottom) shows how to determine whether or not the attic has enough headroom for a conversion.

Ventilation. Measure the depth of the existing rafters to see if there is enough room for fiberglass insulation plus a 2-in. air space above the insulation.

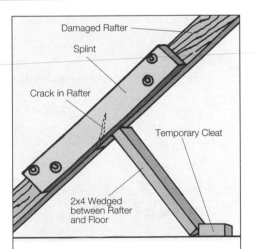

Rafters. Push a damaged rafter back into place and use a splint of lumber (it must be the same dimension as the rafter) to reinforce it. Extend the splint well beyond the damaged wood.

be used to straighten a rafter, but if this does not work, the rafter may have to be jacked into place. This is a job for a professional.

Floor Framing. Check the attic floor joists for damage and sag (use the same technique used for checking rafters). Sags usually are due to insufficient support rather than under-sized joists. If joists overlap near the center of the house, they must be supported by a wall or a beam directly underneath. But if part of that support has been removed, as is sometimes done when two small rooms are combined into one large one, the joists above might sag.

Structural support must continue all the way to the foundation, so check the basement or crawl space to see if support is missing there. If the house was built correctly, you will find a beam or another wall directly beneath the support wall. If you do not see one, a builder or an engineer can determine the proper combination of beams and/or posts required for proper support.

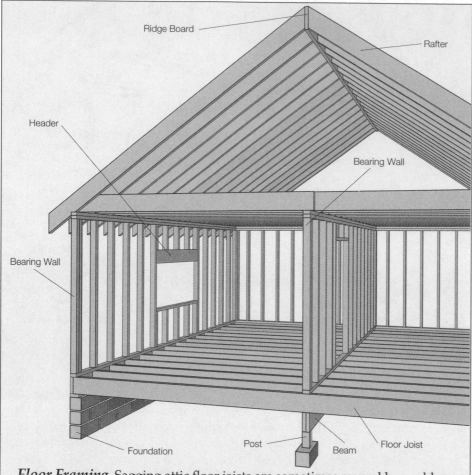

Floor Framing. Sagging attic floor joists are sometimes caused by problems found elsewhere in the house. Check that all loads transfer to the foundation.

Water Leakage. Inspect the underside of the sheathing and the sides of the rafters for brownish stains that may indicate a leak in the roof. Leaks rarely can be repaired from inside the attic, so count on making them from outside. If you find a stain be sure to investigate further; some stains may be due to an old leak that has since been repaired. If the area feels spongy when probed with a flat-blade screwdriver, the leak is active and must be repaired. Another way to check for leaks is to visit the attic during or just after a hard rain.

Leaks commonly are found around flashing, so check around all places where the roof has been penetrated, such as plumbing vents and chimneys. Replace or repair all suspect flashing.

Insect Problems. Though attics are not infested as easily as wood that is closer to the ground, keep an eye out for signs of powder-post beetles, carpenter ants and nonsubterranean termites. Look for swarming insects, a series of pinholes in the wood, and small, powdery piles of sawdust beneath affected wood. If you suspect an infestation, rap the wood with your knuckles or the handle of a screwdriver. Infested wood makes a different sound than solid wood. Infested areas must be treated by a professional exterminator before work begins.

Water Leakage. From the roof, check all flashing for signs of deterioration and replace faulty pieces. Also, check the underside of the roof sheathing for signs of leaks in the shingles.

Chimney Solutions. As long as combustibles are kept away, an airtight, crack-free chimney can add interest to the decor.

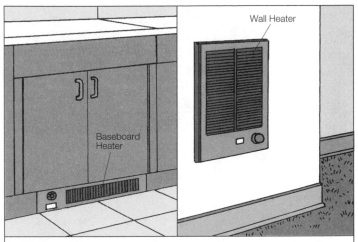

Electric Heaters. When space is tight, a heater can be installed in the kick space of a cabinet (left). A properly sized heater mounted in a wall can heat an attic (right).

Chimney Solutions. It is okay to have an airtight chimney within a living space, as long as you have it inspected by your local fire department. A building inspector can advise you on the relevant building codes. There is not much you can do about moving a chimney, so take some measurements to determine its size and shape and figure out how it fits into your plan. Measure each side of the chimney to determine the amount of headroom you will have when walking around it. Then examine the chimney for cracks in the masonry or loose mortar. Cracks are a particular hazard if the flue does not have a fireproof lining. Joists, rafters or framing that is closer than 2 inches to the chimney at any point is a fire hazard and must be corrected immediately. Make sure all combustible materials are kept well away (unfaced fiberglass is not combustible). If the chimney is made of metal, it must be enclosed. Check local codes for permissible solutions.

Planning for Utilities

Heating the Attic

As part of the preconstruction review of your attic, give some thought to how the space will be heated. Though it might seem tempting simply to cut vents in the ceiling below and let heat rise to the attic, this scheme rarely works. (It also increases noise transmission.) Your heating system can usually be extended to the attic, if you have one of the following systems: forced-air heat (oil, gas or electric), electric baseboard heat, or hydronic baseboard heat.

Electric Heaters. In many cases, an electric baseboard or fan-forced electric heater is enough to supply all the necessary heat and can be installed regardless of the type of heating system that already exists.

Contact a heating contractor for advice before applying for a building permit. Then, if the contractor suggests a particular location for knee walls (to make room for heating ducts), there is time to adjust your plans. It is easiest to rough-in hydronic and forced-air heating systems before the subflooring and knee walls are installed.

Planning the Electrical System

Though it is possible to extend an existing electrical circuit to the attic, doing so may not be the best option. By extending the system, you risk overloading the circuit which probably cannot supply enough power for most conversions. Plan to run at least one new circuit to the attic. If you will be bringing electric heat into the attic, you will need at least two circuits: one for the heat and one for outlets and fixtures. If you are building a home office, plan to add two or more circuits and remember to have a phone line installed (if this is desirable). All attic circuits must meet the same electrical code requirements that govern other living spaces in the house.

In order to accommodate the added electrical load, service to the house must be at least 100 amperes. If your house has 200-ampere service, as most newer homes do, adding the new circuits is easy. However, most homes built before 1941 have two-wire electric service which may limit the number and type of electrical appliances that can be used (newer houses have three-wire service). Consult a licensed electrician to determine whether or not the present system can be added to, modified or upgraded.

Planning the Plumbing System

Water Supply. If your water comes from a well, the ability of the system to support an attic bathroom is determined by the pump and the capacity of the well. A plumbing system supplied by municipal sources generally can accommodate the addition of a small attic bathroom. Because the water heater is probably quite a distance from the attic, you might want to add a point-of-use water heater. These units essentially are miniature boilers that operate on demand. They are small enough to fit beneath the sink

Water Supply. This electric water heater fits under a sink and provides hot water quickly.

or in a storage cabinet. Check with a plumber for information on the availability, power requirements and capacity of these units.

Drainage and Venting. The drainage of waste water and sewage is done through a network of pipes that leads to the sewer or septic tank. In order for these pipes to drain freely, they must be connected to a system of vent pipes that lead up to and through the roof. New fixtures in an attic bathroom usually can tap into the existing system if the bathroom location is planned accordingly. Try to locate the new bathroom as close as possible to existing drain lines. The best location, however, may depend on the direction in which the attic floor joists run. It is best to run drain lines parallel to the joists, so you can avoid having to cut through, and weaken, the joists.

Who Will Do the Work?

Building codes usually allow a homeowner to work on or add to every part of his or her own house, including the plumbing and electrical systems. However, depending on the magnitude of the project, you may want to turn part or all of the work over to a professional. In addition, if you are borrowing money for the project, the lender may require a professional to

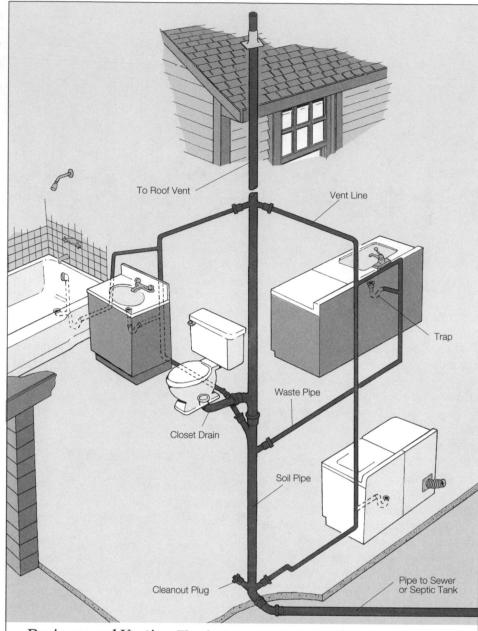

To Roof Vent

Vent Line

Trap

Waste Pipe

Closet Drain

Soil Pipe

Cleanout Plug

Pipe to Sewer or Septic Tank

Drainage and Venting. The drain, waste, vent (DWV) system transports waste from fixtures and appliances to the sewer or septic tank.

complete certain parts of the job. Be sure to question lenders on their particular policies.

If you want someone else to do all the work, including locating and negotiating with each specialty contractor (the plumber and the carpet installer, for example), then hire a builder or general contractor. A builder generally works with his/her own team of specialists, while a general contractor works with various independent specialists. You may choose to take on the role of general

contractor—that means the job of hiring each specialist is in your hands. Working as the general contractor sometimes saves money but can be surprisingly time-consuming.

Getting Bids. Screen each professional before hiring them to work on your house. Ask for references and call several people for whom he or she recently worked. The larger the job, the more important it is to shop around, so get at least three bids for every phase of work. Keep in mind that the lowest bid is not always the best deal. Be confident that the professional can do the job when and how you want it and get all agreements in writing. To ensure that all parties understand exactly what the job entails and can bid accordingly, provide a simple set of plans or sketches to all bidders, including each type and grade of material required.

As the job moves along, you might decide to make some minor design changes. If so, talk to the contractor and come to an agreement on the cost of the change. Then put it in writing. This is called a change order and helps to prevent misunderstandings between contractor and homeowner.

Abiding by Building Codes

Building regulations have been around since at least 2000 BC. when the Code of Hammurabi mandated death to the son of a builder whose building collapses and kills the son of its owner. Codes these days are not quite so severe but they do have something in common with their predecessor in that they reflect the fundamental duty of government to protect the general health, safety and welfare of its citizens.

Attic construction is covered by the same building codes that apply to work done elsewhere in the house. The codes are published in book form. You may be able to purchase the book (or books) from your local building department. They sometimes can be found in the reference section of the local library.

Knowing the Codes

The codes in your community might cover everything from the way the house is used to the materials you can use for building or remodeling it. Some codes prohibit the attic of a two-story house from being used for living space unless extra steps are taken to protect it from fire hazard. There are several types of code that

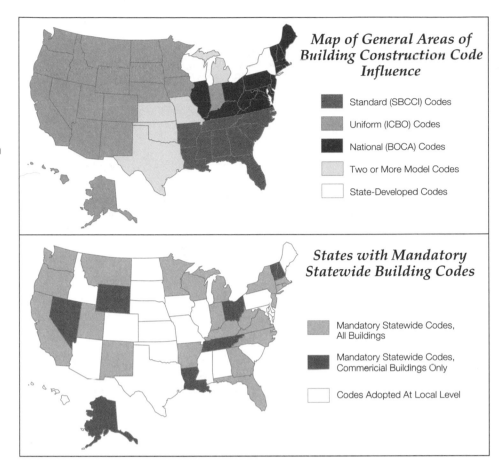

Map of General Areas of Building Construction Code Influence

- Standard (SBCCI) Codes
- Uniform (ICBO) Codes
- National (BOCA) Codes
- Two or More Model Codes
- State-Developed Codes

States with Mandatory Statewide Building Codes

- Mandatory Statewide Codes, All Buildings
- Mandatory Statewide Codes, Commericial Buildings Only
- Codes Adopted At Local Level

About Building Codes

Not all of the United States is covered by the same building codes. In fact each state, county, city and town adopt those codes that best suit local building conditions. References to the building codes in this book are to the 1992 edition of the "One- and Two-Family Dwelling Code" published by The Council of American Building Officials (CABO). Though this code is widely recognized, not all towns have adopted it, and those that have might use an earlier or later version. Before you build, check with local building officials to determine the specific codes used in your area.

you must be aware of when tackling an attic conversion. Depending on its complexity some or all may affect your project.

Building Code. This covers such things as the suitability of construction materials, the span of floor joists, the amount of insulation needed in a ceiling, the type and number of fasteners used to fasten sheathing, and the amount of light and ventilation necessary to provide a healthy living space. Building codes also cover some aspects of installing plumbing and wiring.

Mechanical Code. The installation of heating and cooling equipment (including ducts), wood stoves and chimneys is covered here.

Plumbing Code. This type of code contains rules for the installation of water supply and drain/waste/vent (DWV) systems, as well as related systems.

Energy Codes. In response to energy shortages in the 1970s many municipalities instituted codes that map out minimum requirements for window glazing, insulation and general energy efficiency.

Electrical Code. This code covers the proper installation of household electrical equipment and wiring systems. The National Electric Code, unlike most other codes, pertains to the entire country.

Other Codes. Your community also may have adopted some types of fire prevention codes, accessibility codes (requiring barrier-free access to buildings), or special-construction codes (such as those requiring earthquake-resistant construction).

Following the Codes

Three regional and one national organization have developed different "model" codes. These model codes serve as the basis for most state and local codes.

■ The Uniform Building Code is published by the International Conference of Building Officials (ICBO).

■ The Standard Building Code is published by the Southern Building Code Congress International (SBCCI).

■ The National Code (despite the name is essentially a regional code like the others) is published by the Building Officials and Code Administrators International (BOCA).

■ The One- and Two-Family Dwelling Code is published by the Council of American Building Officials (CABO).

Each state decides which model codes to follow. In some cases a state may adopt two model codes and let towns pick the ones they want to use. That is why codes sometimes vary from community to community within the same state. If you have a choice, you probably will find the CABO code easiest to understand because it is more specific about what can—and cannot—be done. The other model codes, however, offer more latitude for solving unusual problems that may be encountered. To determine the combination of codes that apply in your area start by inquiring locally.

City or Town Level. Check with the local building and zoning department, if there is one, or with the housing department or town clerk.

County Level. If you live outside the boundaries of a city or town, check with the county clerk or county commission.

State Level. If you cannot find a city or county office that covers building codes, check with the state offices. Codes may be administered by the departments of housing, community affairs, building standards, or even by the labor department (sometimes they regulate builders). You also might check with the state fire marshal or state energy office.

Do You Need a Permit?

Permits and inspections are a way of enforcing the building codes. Essentially, a permit is the license that gives you permission to do the work, and an inspection ensures that you did the work according to code. Usually a permit is not necessary for minor repair or remodeling work, but you may need one for adding a dormer, extending the water supply and DWV system, or adding an electrical circuit. You almost always need one to convert an attic to living space.

Having an Inspection

When a permit is required, a city or county building inspector usually has to examine the work. He or she checks to see that the work meets or exceeds the building codes. At the time you obtain a permit, ask about the inspection schedule. With small projects an inspector might only require a final inspection; with a larger project several intermediate inspections may be necessary before a final inspection is done. In any case, it is your job to call for the inspection, not the inspector's job to figure out when you might be ready for a visit.

Zoning Ordinances

Another type of regulation that can affect an attic conversion is called a zoning ordinance. Some residential zoning ordinances are designed to keep multi-family homes out of single-family neighborhoods. If your attic plans call for the addition of a small bathroom and a separate outside entrance, local zoning officials might interpret this as an attempt to add a rental unit and deny a permit. However, if you change the plans to incorporate an internal stair, your attic no longer appears to be a rental and your plans, barring other problems, probably will be approved. Zoning ordinances sometimes restrict the height of a house or your ability to change its exterior. This might affect your plans to add a dormer to the attic. If you want to convert the attic to a bedroom, zoning ordinances might require you to enlarge your septic system (another bedroom implies another resident, which in turn implies increased demand on the septic system). Though most attic conversions do not run afoul of zoning ordinances, it is always a good idea to check with local officials before any work is done.

Obtaining a Permit

Depending on the scope of the work, a permit application must include the following items:

Legal Description of Property. You can get this from city or county records or directly from your deed.

Drawing of Proposed Changes. This drawing need not be done by an architect, but must clearly show the structural changes you plan to make. It also must identify the type and dimension of all materials. Most building departments accept attic plans drawn by a homeowner as long as the details are clearly labeled. Note the dimensions and span of existing and new materials.

Site Plan Drawing. This shows the position of the house on the lot, and the approximate location of adjacent houses. It also shows the location of the well and septic system, if any.

PLANNING & DESIGN

As far as an attic conversion goes, many key decisions to be made involve stairways and general headroom. With those problems solved you are ready to design a room that makes the most of space-efficient furnishings.

Gaining Access

Few houses are designed with an attic conversion in mind so access routes typically are rudimentary. In some cases the only access is through a hatch plate tucked into the ceiling of a closet. Other houses may have pull-down stairs, but these cannot legally be used to reach a finished attic. Because a pull-down stair fits into an opening that is only about 26 inches wide, the opening has to be enlarged to accommodate the width of a standard stairway. A standard, straight-run stairway is about 3 feet wide and 12 to 13 feet long without landings (allow at least 3 feet for a landing at the top and bottom). Building codes require a minimum vertical clearance of 6 feet 8 inches at all points on the stairs.

Location. First make two decisions: Where will the stair start and where will it end? Look for underused space below the attic. If a wall is removed from between two small rooms the resulting larger room possibly can provide the needed space. A bedroom closet might be changed into a stairwell. You might even decide to sacrifice a small room in order to gain

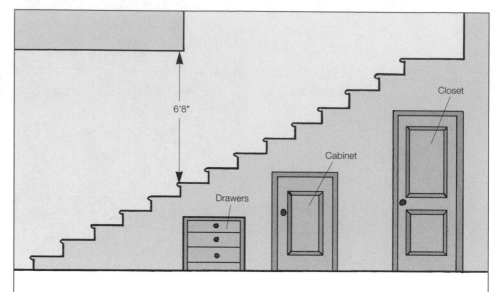

Gaining Access. Code requires that stairs have at least 6 ft. 8 in. of headroom measured vertically at the front edge of the steps. Where headroom is less than 6 ft. 8 in., the attic floor must be cut away. Use the stairwell for storage.

suitable access to the attic (if doing so results in a net gain of floor space).

Using the Roof Angle. Once a starting place is found you can determine where the stairway will end. Ample headroom at the top of the stair is not always easy to find in a room that has ceilings that slope to the floor. Terminating the top of the stair near the center of the attic provides the greatest headroom above. However, you can place the stair closer to attic walls if its angle follows the angle of the roof. Another trick is to build a dormer over the stairwell; not only does a dormer provide a suitable design, it also provides the stair with plenty of natural light.

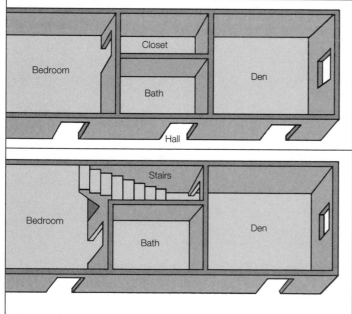

Location. Look for underused spaces beneath the attic, or consider changing room configurations. Here, a stair replaces a closet.

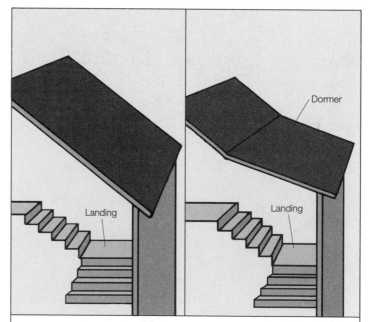

Using the Roof Angle. To conserve space, arrange the stair so that it descends as it steps towards the eaves (left). You can move the stairs even closer to the eaves by building a dormer to gain headroom (right).

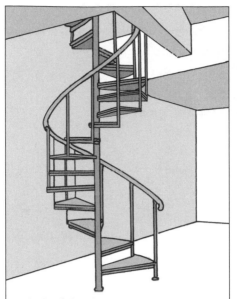

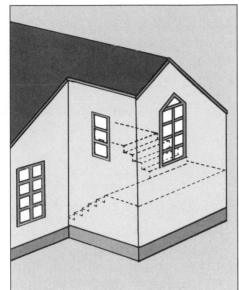

Straight-Run Stairs. This common stair is the easiest stair to build but requires a long, straight stretch of space. It can be completely enclosed or one side can remain partially or fully open.

Spiral Stairs. This is the most compact design but often is difficult for children and elderly to navigate. Its use may not be allowed in your area so check building codes.

Stair Tower. Building a separate structure to house the stair is the most expensive approach but may be the only solution in some situations.

Types of Stairs

Straight-Run Stairs. The standard straight-run stairway is about 3 feet wide and at least 11 feet long, excluding a landing at the top and bottom. Finding room for something that takes up this much space is not easy. Start by looking for seldom used rooms beneath the attic—perhaps one can be put to a better use as home for a new stairway.

Spiral Stairs. From a purely visual standpoint there is nothing quite like a set of spiral stairs. They can be installed in a space as small as 4 feet in diameter but may be difficult for some people to use (particularly the elderly). Also note that it is challenging, if not impossible, to get furniture up spiral stairs. An advantage of using a spiral stair, however, is that it can be purchased as a kit and assembled on site rather than built from scratch. Check your local building codes; some restrict the use of spiral stairs.

Stair Tower. If there absolutely is no room for a stairway inside the house consider installing an outside stair tower. Like all others additions, a stair tower requires a separate foundation. It also has a considerable impact on the appearance of the house so you might want to enlist the help of a designer or architect when considering the project.

L- and U-Shaped Stairs. If there is not room for a straight-run stair, consider L- or U-shaped stairs. Though they are harder to build, these stairs are more compact and do not require the length of uninterrupted floor space needed by straight-run stairs.

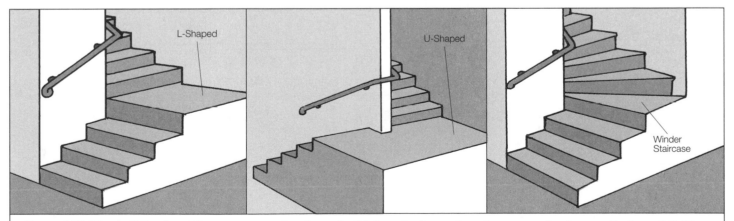

L- and U-Shaped Stairs. These stairs are harder to build, but don't require a long stretch of space. L-shaped (left), U-shaped (middle), and winders (right) must be code approved.

It is helpful to know the size of various fixtures and furniture so you can map out appropriate arrangements in limited space. Remember too, that you have to get everything upstairs somehow. Double beds and spiral stairs, for example, do not mix.

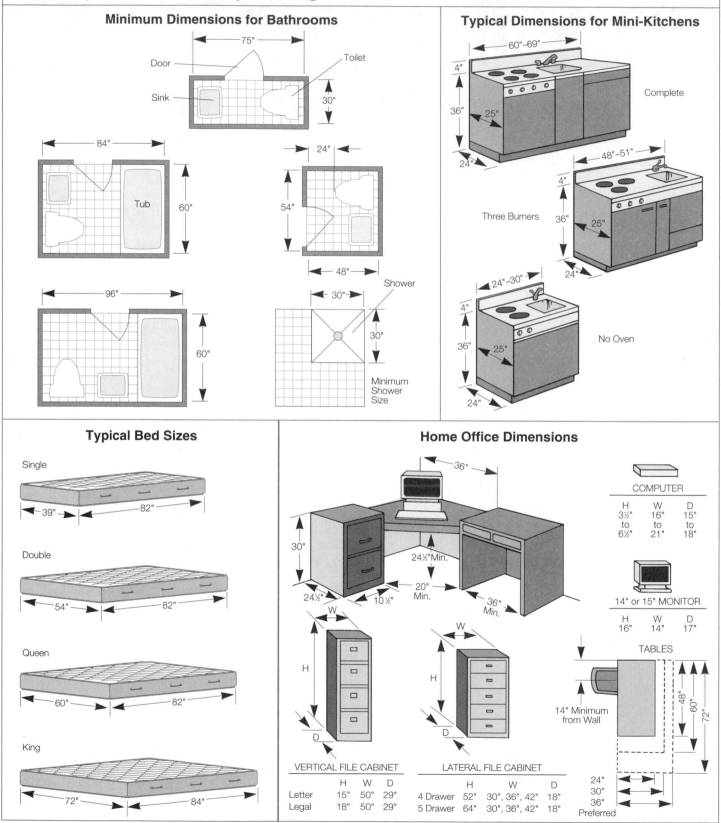

Minimum Dimensions for Bathrooms

Typical Dimensions for Mini-Kitchens

Typical Bed Sizes

Home Office Dimensions

VERTICAL FILE CABINET

	H	W	D
Letter	15"	50"	29"
Legal	18"	50"	29"

LATERAL FILE CABINET

	H	W	D
4 Drawer	52"	30", 36", 42"	18"
5 Drawer	64"	30", 36", 42"	18"

COMPUTER

H	W	D
3½" to 6½"	16" to 21"	15" to 18"

14" or 15" MONITOR

H	W	D
16"	14"	17"

Finding Attic Space Savers. Wherever possible use the areas with reduced headroom for activities that do not require standing.

Finding Attic Space Savers

If space is at a premium shop for space-efficient appliances and dual-use furnishings (such as a table that expands to provide an extra work surface). Place desks and seating areas against knee walls to make the most of reduced headroom; book-shelves also work well in this area.

Using Knee Wall Storage

If you are clever, you will find a way to use every ounce of storage space behind the knee walls. This wedge-shaped space is good for storing everything from files and office sup-plies to shoes and clothing. Individ-ual drawers and rolling bins that pull into the room can be built into the knee walls.

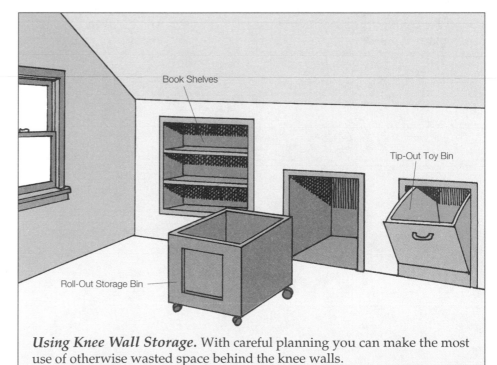

Book Shelves

Tip-Out Toy Bin

Roll-Out Storage Bin

Using Knee Wall Storage. With careful planning you can make the most use of otherwise wasted space behind the knee walls.

Installing Floors & Floor Coverings

There is no limit to the kind of floor you can install in the attic. Carpeting is particularly suitable for bedrooms, and sheet vinyl is as suitable for an attic kitchenette as it is for the main kitchen. It is best to use hardwood (or vinyl) in a home office to reduce the dust and static electricity that plays havoc with sensitive electronic equipment such as computers and fax machines.

Carpeting can be installed directly over most plywood subfloors. Sheet vinyl, however, must be installed over an extra-smooth surface to eliminate the likelihood of imperfections "telegraphing" through the vinyl. Underlayment plywood has a sanded surface that is smooth enough to use beneath vinyl floors. If you opt to use a separate layer of underlayment instead, use 1/4-inch-thick luaun plywood or Masonite. The type of finished flooring you choose affects decisions to be made early in the project (such as stair planning), so make your selection as soon as possible.

Controlling Noise

Most bedrooms are upstairs for a reason: The quiet uses of a bedroom should not be interrupted by activities taking place in the attic. Converting

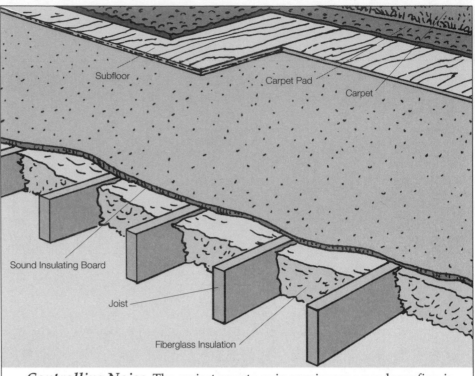

Subfloor · Carpet Pad · Carpet · Sound Insulating Board · Joist · Fiberglass Insulation

Controlling Noise. The easiest way to gain maximum soundproofing is to place fiberglass insulation and soundboard beneath the subfloor. Wall-to-wall carpeting and a good-quality carpet pad complete the system.

an attic to living space short circuits this design, so you may want to consider soundproofing the floor. Note, however, that the word "soundproofing" is something of a misnomer. Noise can only be reduced, not eliminated.

Thick wall-to-wall carpeting and a high-quality pad absorb much of the sound that otherwise passes through the floor. For additional sound control add sound deadening material in the middle of a three-layer subfloor. Fiberglass insulation can be added between joist bays. This is about all you can do to reduce sound transmission without adding considerable expense to the project.

PREPARING THE ATTIC SPACE

As with most major remodeling projects there is much to do before getting to the things that actually show progress. You may have to accomplish certain tasks beforehand, such as removing existing walls to make room for a new stair, or reinforcing the attic floor to make it safe for walking. In any case, careful planning ensures your success.

Removing Walls

Nearly every remodeling project calls for the removal of existing walls or surfaces before the rest of the work can begin. It might seem that attic conversions would be an exception to this rule, but usually this is not the case. Sometimes walls beneath the attic have to be removed to make way for a new stair. Or perhaps you have to remove the existing attic flooring to get at and strengthen the floor joists. You may have to demolish existing attic storage to clear space for the new room. Whatever the reason, demolition is likely to be a part of your project.

Putting a house together can be hazardous, but taking one apart, even partially, calls for particular vigilance. Many accidents occur simply because people expect demolition to be easy (it is not!), so they are not as careful as they might be. In addition to the general safety tips listed at the front of this book, pay particular attention to the guidelines below.

Removing Nails

There probably are a lot of nails to remove and when they are removed correctly a potential hazard is eliminated. Money can be saved by reusing some old materials such as trim and molding (nails cannot be reused).

Finishing Nails. It is best to remove the molding itself first and then the nails. To remove the molding without damaging it, place a scrap of wood behind the pry bar (to protect the wall surface) and gradually pry the molding away from the wall. If the nails poke through the front of the molding use a pry bar to remove them. If the nails stay in the molding—and they often do—the best way to remove them is with nippers. Grasp the shank of the nail and lever it from the back side of the molding (in a pinch you can do the same thing with side cutters). The beauty of this technique is that there are no nailholes to patch; the nail pulls through the back of the wood without disturbing the face.

Large Nails. Nails are not always easy to remove and sometimes the best you can do is to cut a nail flush with the surface of the wood. This is another job for nippers. Grasp the nail as if you were going to pull it out,

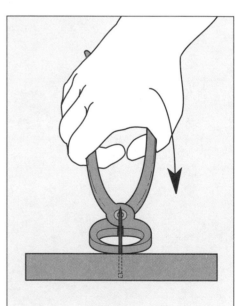

Finishing Nails. Grasp the nail at the surface and use the nippers to pull it through the backside of the wood. This minimizes damage to the face of the stock.

Demolition Safety

■ Wear work boots. Not only do they help protect your feet from debris, they also shield your ankles from the scrapes and cuts commonly caused by demolition work. Wear long pants to protect your legs.

■ Wear leather work gloves that have cuffs to protect your wrists. Canvas gloves can be pierced easily and are not good for this type of work.

■ Wear a dust mask and change it frequently. Even a small amount of demolition kicks a lot of dust into the air.

■ Always wear safety glasses—particularly when using nippers to cut nails.

■ Remove nails from pieces of wood or pound them flat as you remove the wood itself. This prevents you from stepping on them as work progresses.

■ Frequently clean up the area and remove excess debris.

■ Proceed methodically, removing materials piece by piece and layer by layer.

■ Never remove a wall until you know whether or not it is a bearing wall. Always assume that there is wiring or plumbing in the wall even if it is not evident.

■ If you encounter a material suspected of containing asbestos, contact your health or consumer product agencies at the local or state level. Asbestos is a fibrous mineral that at one time was used as an ingredient in a variety of construction products. Now it is considered to be a serious health hazard and experts are unable to provide assurances that any level of exposure to it is completely safe. Houses younger than about 20 years old probably do not contain asbestos. An older house may or may not contain it. Remodeling work can damage asbestos-containing materials and cause asbestos fibers to be released into the air. Places where you might find asbestos include: around pipes and furnaces; in some vinyl flooring materials; in some ceiling tiles; in exterior roofing and siding shingles; in some drywall; troweled or sprayed around pipes, ducts and beams; in patching compounds or textured paints; and in door gaskets on stoves, furnaces and ovens. The repair or removal of products that contain asbestos must be done by a trained contractor.

You can get a lot done with a hammer but having a selection of demolition tools on hand speeds up the work and makes it safer. As an added incentive for buying them, these tools are relatively inexpensive.

Claw Hammer. A 16-ounce claw hammer that has a steel handle and a rubber or leather grip is handy to have around. Its steel handle is practically indestructible and the claw makes quick work of removing medium-sized nails. The claw hammer also can be used to strike the head of a pry bar.

Pry Bar. Pry bars are demolition workhorses. They come in a variety of shapes and sizes from 8 to 18 inches long. Though a 12-inch or 13-inch bar handles many jobs, it is best to have several sizes on hand (including an 8-inch bar for prying small moldings away from the wall). Most bars have a notch at one or both ends for removing nails and often can reach into places the claw of a hammer cannot.

Wrecking Bar. A wrecking bar (sometimes called a crow bar, ripping bar or pinch bar) is a heavy steel bar bent into a U-shape at one end and flattened at the other. Its length, 24 to 30 inches, provides extra leverage for prying apart layers of nailed wood and nudging framed walls into place. It also provides extra reach for pulling plaster from walls.

Nippers. Nippers are the ideal tool for removing a nail when its head has broken off; other nail removing tools cannot get a grip in such cases. Likewise, nippers are handy for removing finishing nails. The tool also can snip small nails flush to the surface of the wood. Long-handled models provide the best leverage.

Cat's Paw. A cat's paw is used to remove nails. It has a curved, slightly pointed head with a V-shaped groove cut into it. When hit with a hammer the head is driven below the surface of the wood to dig under nailheads, even if they have been countersunk.

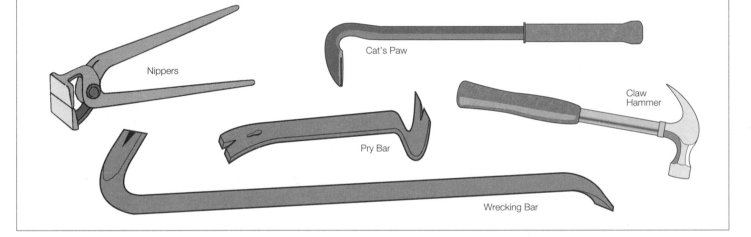

Nippers

Cat's Paw

Claw Hammer

Pry Bar

Wrecking Bar

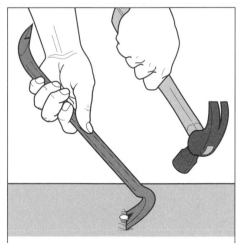

Large Nails. Use a pry bar and hammer to remove nails that have sunk below the surface of the wood.

then squeeze the nippers as hard as you can. Small nails shear off easily. However, the shank of larger nails (about 10d and above) may not yield to one bite of the nippers. If this is the case, grip the nail hard as described above, then rotate the nippers a quarter turn and grip again. This creates a score line on the nail. Move the nippers higher on the exposed nail shank and bend the nail over, shearing it at the score line.

Use a pry bar to pull nails from framing lumber. Place the notch at a slight angle to the surface of the wood, then strike the pry bar just hard enough to drive the notch under the

head of the nail. You may need to hit it a second time to ensure a good grip on the nail shank. Use one smooth motion to lever out the nail. A cat's paw is used in a similar fashion.

Removing Drywall or Plaster

Simply put, a wall is an assembly of parts. To get rid of a wall, remove the parts one by one, layer by layer. This process is the reverse of building a wall. Begin with the wall covering and go from there.

Removing Drywall

The most common indoor wall surface is 1/2-inch-thick drywall. The material itself is not particularly tough but the number of nails used to attach it to the framing make it awkward and messy to remove. You may be inclined simply to bash the wall with a hammer, but this is the slowest, messiest, most dangerous and least effective way to remove drywall (though it may be fairly satisfying if you are having a rough day). Use the following method instead.

1 Protecting the Area. Remove all furniture from the area and use a canvas tarp to cover the floor in the immediate vicinity. Confine the very fine dust created by drywall removal to a relatively small area by using plastic sheets to close off adjacent doorways.

2 Turning off Power. Turn off power to outlets, switches and fixtures in the wall to be removed. Remove cover plates, switches and outlets from electrical boxes that will be relocated. A small piece of electrical tape placed over nearby receptacles keeps out dust and debris.

3 Locating Studs. Use a utility knife to score the drywall, running it around the perimeter of the piece you wish to remove. Locate the wall studs; there are various ways to find them. Using an electronic stud finder is a simple matter of pressing a button and slowly dragging the device across the wall. You also can probe for studs using a hammer and nail. The typical spacing for 2x4 studs is 16 inches center-to-center so once you find one stud you can figure out where the rest of them ought to be.

4 Locating Nails. Use a magnet or magnetic-type stud finder to locate the nails that hold the drywall to the studs. Chances are the nail pattern in one stud is similar to the pattern in others so you may be able to guess where the rest of the nails are once you have located them in a few studs.

5 Pulling off Drywall. Use a hammer and short scrap of copper plumbing pipe to punch a hole around each nail. This isolates it from the surrounding drywall. Remove the drywall by pulling it away from the wall. Then use a pry bar or hammer to pull nails from the framing.

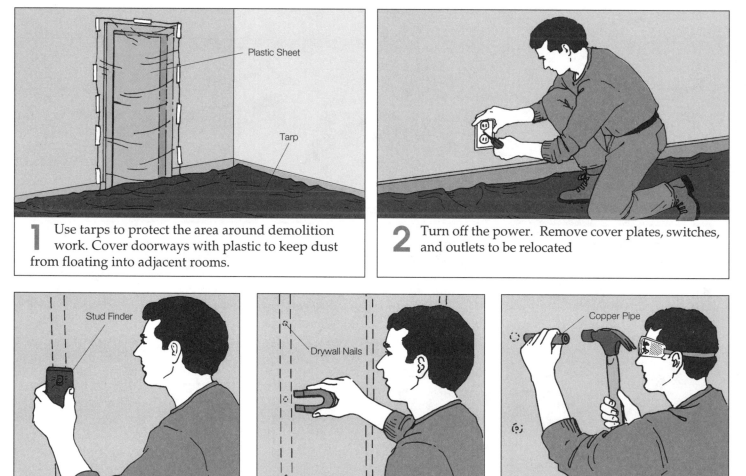

1 Use tarps to protect the area around demolition work. Cover doorways with plastic to keep dust from floating into adjacent rooms.

2 Turn off the power. Remove cover plates, switches, and outlets to be relocated

3 Use a stud finder to locate a stud, then measure along the wall to locate others.

4 With a magnet, locate the drywall nails and mark their locations with a pencil.

5 Over each nail, strike a copper pipe with a hammer to cut through the drywall. Remove the sheet of drywall and pull the nails.

Removing Plaster & Lath

Stripping plaster from a wall is dirty work no matter how it is done. Some people prefer to cut it away in chunks using a circular saw set to make a shallow cut. Others find it easier just to batter the plaster with a hammer, pull it away in chunks and pry away the lath using a crowbar.

Removing Framing

There are two basic types of walls in every house and it is essential that you identify each one before attempting to remove it. If you skip this step you risk injury to yourself and serious damage to your house.

Bearing Walls. A wall that supports structural loads (such as a floor, a roof or another wall above) and helps to transmit those loads to the foundation of the house is a bearing wall. Except for gable walls, most exterior walls are bearing walls. Usually a wall that runs lengthwise through the center of a house is a bearing wall and joists along each side of the house rest on it. Bearing walls sometimes can be spotted from the attic; they are the ones holding up the ends of joists (particularly where two sets of joist ends overlap). You also

may be able to identify bearing walls from the basement. Look for walls that rest atop a beam or a basement wall. If you are not sure about the kind of wall you are dealing with, the safest thing to do is assume that it is a bearing wall. In order to remove bearing walls safely, you have to identify all the loads involved and provide alternate support for them. Seek professional advice from a builder or engineer when a bearing wall must be removed.

Non-Bearing Walls. Non-bearing walls, also called partition walls, support only the wall covering attached to them. Usually a non-bearing wall can be removed without affecting the structural integrity of the house. If a wall does not support joist ends and does not lie directly beneath a post, it may be a non-bearing wall. Walls that run parallel to ceiling joists usually are non-bearing walls.

Wiring and Plumbing. Before removing a wall, check the area immediately above and beneath it from the attic and basement, if possible. Look for wires, pipes or ducts that lead into the wall. There is no way to tell for sure how big the job is until the drywall or plaster is pulled from at least one side of the wall.

Removing Plaster & Lath. Pulling plaster from a wall is messy business. Wear gloves for protection from splinters.

Wiring is easy to relocate but plumbing supply piping (hot and cold water pipes) is more difficult. Plumbing vent pipes are trickier still, primarily because of code requirements that restrict their placement. Heating ducts and drain pipes are the toughest of all to relocate. Consult a professional if you are unsure of what to do. With luck, the wall you open up contains nothing but dust.

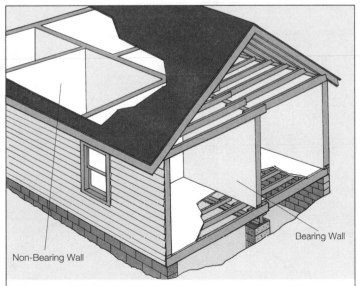

Non-Bearing Wall

Bearing Wall

Bearing Walls. Before removing a wall determine whether or not it is a bearing wall. Look for clues such as lapped joists above. Walls that are parallel to the attic joists usually are not load bearing.

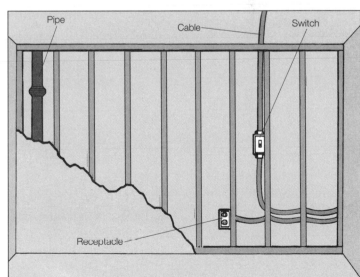

Pipe

Cable

Switch

Receptacle

Wiring and Plumbing. Plumbing and wiring are two commonly encountered obstructions within a wall. Examine the wall from the attic and the basement to determine their exact locations.

1 Use a sledge hammer to loosen one stud at a time. Use light force; you will not be able to reuse the lumber if it becomes damaged.

2 Twist each stud away from the top wall plate. Be careful not to step on nails that protrude through the bottom plate.

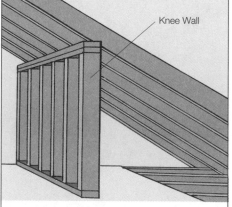

3 Use a wrecking bar to lever up the bottom plate. Remove all debris promptly to avoid tripping over it.

Removing a Non-Bearing Wall

1 Loosening the Studs. After stripping the wall covering from both sides and relocating utilities, use a sledge to force the bottom of each stud away from the nails that hold it in place. Proceed cautiously until you get the feel for how much force is required.

2 Removing Studs. Once the bottom is loose, grasp the stud and push it first sideways, and then outwards and back and forth to work the top nails loose until you can remove the stud. Cut and remove one stud at a time or you will find yourself assaulted by a dangling row of severed 2x4s. As you work, hammer over nails that protrude from the bottom plate. This way they cannot puncture your foot as you work on the next stud.

3 Prying off Plates. Use a crowbar to remove the end studs, and then the top and bottom plates. Nails may be located anywhere along the length of each end stud.

Removing Collar Ties & Knee Walls

Just to be on the safe side always consider the knee walls and collar ties that you find in an unfinished attic to be structural elements. Though either feature may be nonstructural, it is a good idea to be cautious when the structural integrity of your house is at stake. If the success of an attic renovation absolutely depends on moving collar ties or structural knee walls, consult an engineer or an architect for advice.

Collar Ties. The weight of the roofing, along with wind and snow loads, pushes down on the rafters. Collar ties hold ridge board and rafters together, and the attic floor joists keep the exterior walls from being pushed outward. The position, dimension, and number of collar ties are factors that determine their effectiveness.

Knee Walls. Sometimes knee walls are used to support rafters at mid-span. If a house is particularly wide, for example, the rafters would have to be unusually large to reach from the ridge to outer wall. With a knee wall, however, the span of the rafters can, in effect, be cut in half and that means a smaller dimension of lumber can be used. The knee wall usually transfers the load to a wall or beam beneath. By moving the knee wall, not only do you change the effective span of the rafters, but you also might transfer loads to a part of the house that cannot handle them.

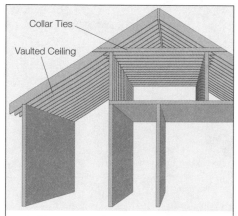

Collar Ties. These pieces of 1-by or 2-by lumber are located at the top third of the space between floor and ridge.

Knee Walls. These short walls may be nonstructural, or they may support rafters at the middle of their span.

Reusing Materials

You can reduce the cost of remodeling by reusing materials, but you have to be selective. It makes little sense to spend 30 minutes painstakingly removing nails from a piece of wood that costs a dollar or two to replace. In general it is worth your time to salvage trim and molding (particularly if it's hardwood), solid wood and plywood paneling, plywood sheathing that is larger than 3 feet square, and siding that is in good condition. Take time to recover materials you may need later in the course of the project. Old tongue-and-groove sheathing boards, for example, often are useful as patching material because new tongue-and-groove stock probably differs slightly in thickness and width. Electrical outlets and switches can be reused but they are so inexpensive that many people prefer to replace them.

If you have the room, set aside anything you think you might need later and hang on to it until the project is complete. Anything you do not end up using can be hauled to the dump afterwards. Materials generally not worth saving include drywall, nails, and framing lumber that is less than 3 feet long. For safety reasons do not reinstall used single-conductor wiring in an electrical circuit. As for galvanized pipe, there are various places for it in your garden but do not bother to reconnect it to your household water system. Lengths of copper water pipe can sometimes be used again, but must be cleaned around the joints.

Planning the Logistics

Turning your attic into a livable space calls for a surprisingly large volume of materials and introduces some unusual logistical issues. Even small projects require flooring, lengths of baseboard, sheets of drywall and buckets of joint compound. Getting all of these materials into the attic can be tricky. If you are opening a gable end for new windows check with materials suppliers to see if they use a boom truck for the main delivery. This type of truck has a miniature crane that lifts materials directly into the attic. If your order is large enough, they might not charge you for this extra service.

Building a Catwalk

Before you spend much time working in the attic, nail some temporary flooring to the joists for your own safety. This catwalk need not be more than two or three feet wide, but it must run the length of the attic. Its purpose is to prevent you from tripping on the floor joists as you prepare the attic for construction. More than one do-it-yourselfer has ended up with bruised shins and a big hole to patch after accidentally stepping through the ceiling of the room below. Always secure the temporary flooring with enough nails to prevent it from moving as you walk. Never lay it loosely.

Transporting Materials

Lumber. If your attic requires support beams, joists and rafter stock, it probably needs them in unwieldy lengths. The most direct route to the attic is not always the best when you are carrying a 12-foot 2x8. Look for the route that has the fewest turns. If you buy longer lengths than needed cut them to approximate length on the ground before taking them upstairs. You may be able to slide lumber piece by piece through a gable-end window.

Subflooring and Paneling. Plywood and particleboard are available in 4x8-foot sheets. This makes them awkward to carry through the house; particularly up the stairs. Precut the panels on the ground, if possible, to fit as needed in the attic. Short knee walls are common in attic renovation projects and offer a good chance to apply this technique. Subflooring panels must be used full size, however, to maintain their structural integrity. If you need a lot of them, take them up in small groups over a period of several days and install each group before bringing in the next one. This does not save you time but it does reduce back strain and mini-mizes concentrated weight on the attic floor.

Drywall. Drywall particularly can be awkward to carry up stairs. It is heavy, relatively fragile and comes in 4x8-foot sheets that turn a stairway into a torture course. One way to ease the chore of carrying them is to use a lifting hook that fits around the bottom of a drywall sheet. If you cannot find one at a local materials supplier make one from scrap metal.

Building a Catwalk. A platform of 1x6s keeps you from stepping through the ceiling. Be sure a joist supports the end of each board.

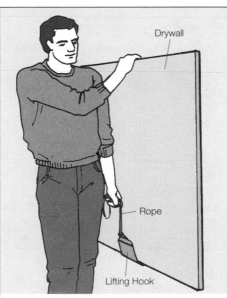

Drywall. Use a metal lifting hook to help carry sheets of drywall or plywood. The rope adjusts to suit your height.

Tub and Shower Units. Getting a tub and shower unit into the attic may take some careful planning. Depending on your project you might be able to use a crane to bring it through the rough opening in the roof just before you frame the dormer, or through a gable end when you frame for a new window. Consider tiling the surround if you cannot get a one-piece unit upstairs. You also may choose to use one of the tub-surround kits designed for remodeling work. These kits are made with interlocking acrylic panels that fold flat for transport.

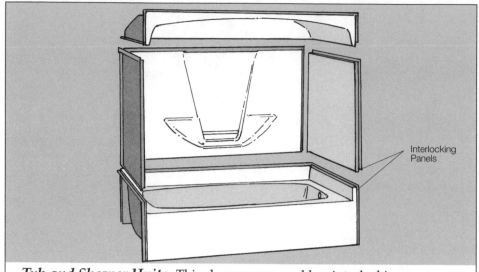

Interlocking Panels

Tub and Shower Units. This shower surround has interlocking parts so it is easy to carry up to the attic. It fits into the 5-ft. space required for a standard tub.

Building Attic Floors

When the attic is turned into living space the ceiling joists for the rooms below suddenly turn into floor joists for your new attic room. Unfortunately ceiling joists are not designed to withstand the loads expected of floor joists so you might have to reinforce them. Do not assume that the existing joists are okay—check them before you proceed with the conversion.

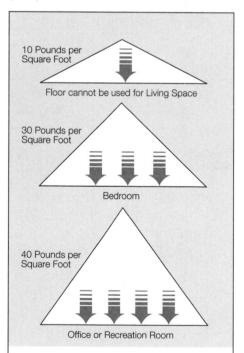

10 Pounds per Square Foot

Floor cannot be used for Living Space

30 Pounds per Square Foot

Bedroom

40 Pounds per Square Foot

Office or Recreation Room

Understanding Floor Loading. Building codes that cover the span of joists are based on the expectation of various loading conditions. Heavier loading calls for deeper joists.

Understanding Floor Loading

All joists are sized to withstand a particular load. In construction, loads are divided into two categories: "Dead" loads are static and account for the weight of the building itself, including lumber and finish materials such as tile or drywall. "Live" loads, on the other hand, are dynamic loads that account for the highly changeable weight of people and furniture. For example, 25 guests dancing the polka at your birthday party, or the 100 gallon aquarium in your son's bedroom. Add the dead loads and the live loads to determine the total load on the joists.

In a home, dead loads usually are figured at 10 pounds per square foot (lbs/psf) of floor space. Live loads vary. Ceiling joists are designed to withstand live loads as small as 10 lbs/psf. Bedroom floor joists must withstand live loads of 30 lbs/psf and joists beneath other attic rooms (such as a home office) must withstand live loads of 40 lbs/psf. The ability of a joist floor to withstand a particular combination of live and dead loads is determined by a variety of factors: the species of wood, the depth and thickness of each joist, the spacing of joists, and the distance between joist supports (called the span). All of these factors combined affect not only the strength of the floor, but also its stiffness. All floors flex somewhat as they are loaded, though floors with properly sized joists do not flex enough to be noticeable. Before you can consult the span tables you must gather some information.

Moving Materials Safely

Always bend your knees and keep your back straight when lifting heavy materials. This may feel awkward at first but it reduces stress on your lower back.

Always get help moving long pieces of lumber. It is easy to damage surrounding walls when maneuvering lengths of lumber by yourself in the confined space of a remodeling project.

Panel products are awkward for one person to move so get help whenever possible.

1 Check the dimension of existing joists by measuring for depth and width. Round up to the nearest whole number.

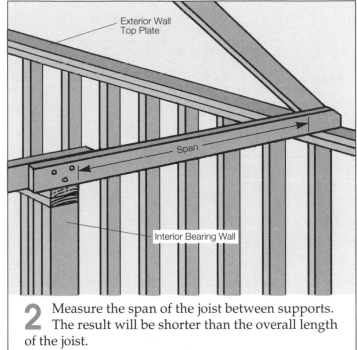

2 Measure the span of the joist between supports. The result will be shorter than the overall length of the joist.

Measuring a Floor for Loading

1 Measuring Joist Dimension. Put on protective gloves and push aside the insulation between a pair of joists. Measure the depth of one joist and round the number to the nearest whole number. For example, 5⅝ inches is rounded up to 6 inches. This is the nominal dimension (the figure used in span tables). Measure the width of the joist and round up that number as well.

2 Figuring Joist Span. The span of a joist is the distance between supports. In most cases, attic joists rest on the outer wall of the house and an interior wall. Measure the distance between supports (you may have to push aside more insulation to get an accurate measurement).

3 Measuring Joist Spacing. The closer the joist spacing, the stronger the floor. Measure across the tops of several joists from centerline to centerline. Check in several places around the attic to see if all the joists have approximately the same spacing.

4 Reading the Charts. Once you have gathered all the information concerning the structural details

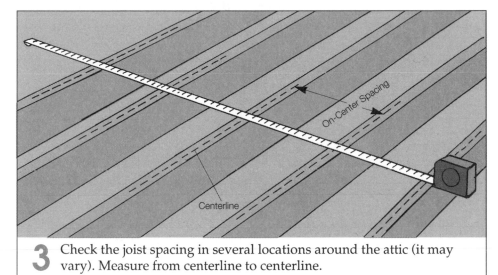

3 Check the joist spacing in several locations around the attic (it may vary). Measure from centerline to centerline.

of the attic floor it is time to consult the charts to determine whether or not the existing floor is strong enough to support a living space. Because the charts found in building code books attempt to account for all the variables that affect floor strength, they can be a little intimidating at first. With a bit of practice, however, you will see how useful they are.

The first chart you need is called "Design Values for Joists and Rafters." It rates the various species of construction woods in terms of their strength (the allowable bending

stress or "Fb") and stiffness (the modulus of elasticity or "E"). The figure you need is the stiffness, so first find the grade stamp on the lumber used for your floor joist. For example, if the grade reads "hemlock-fir in a No. 3 grade," then according to the design values chart this wood has a modulus of 1,200,000 (see chart following page).

Take this figure to the charts labeled "Allowable Spans for Floor Joists" which also are found in the code book. Look for the depth of your joists (in this sample they are 2x6s) on the

Design Values for Joists and Rafters

Species and Grade	Size	Normal Duration	Snow Loading	7 Day Loading	Modulus of Elasticity "E"	Grading Rules
Engelmann Spruce–Alpine Fir (Engelmann Spruce–Logdepole Pine) (Surfaced Dry or Surfaced Green)						
Select Structural		1550	1780	1940	1,300,000	
No. 1 & Appearance		1350	1550	1690	1,300,000	
No. 2	2x4	1100	1260	1380	1,100,000	Western
No. 3		600	690	750	1,000,000	Wood
Stud		600	690	750	1,000,000	Products
Construction		800	920	1000	1,000,000	Association
Standard	2x4	450	520	560	1,000,000	
Utility		200	230	250	1,000,000	
Select Structural		1350	1550	1690	1,300,000	
No. 1 & Appearance	2x5	1150	1320	1440	1,300,000	
No. 2	and	950	1090	1190	1,100,000	
No. 3	Wider	550	630	690	1,000,000	
Stud		550	630	690	1,000,000	
Hem–Fir (Surfaced Dry or Surfaced Green)						
Select Structural		1900	2180	2380	1,500,000	
No. 1 & Appearance		1600	1840	2000	1,500,000	
No. 2	2x4	1350	1550	1690	1,400,000`	Western
No. 3		725	830	910	1,200,000	Wood
Stud		725	830	910	1,200,000	Products
Construction		975	1120	1220	1,200,000	Association
Standard	2x4	550	630	690	1,200,000	
Utility		250	290	310	1,200,000	West Coast
Select Structural		1650	1900	2060	1,500,000	Lumber
No. 1 & Appearance	2x5	1400	1610	1750	1,500,000	Inspection
No. 2	and	1150	1320	1440	1,400,000	Bureau
No. 3	Wider	675	780	840	1,200,000	
Stud		675	780	840	1,200,000	
Hem–Fir (North) (Surfaced Dry or Surfaced Green)						
Select Structural		1800	2070	2250	1,500,000	
No. 1 & Appearance		1550	1780	1940	1,500,000	
No. 2	2x4	1300	1500	1620	1,400,000	
No. 3		700	800	875	1,200,000	
Stud		700	800	875	1,200,000	National
Construction		925	1060	1160	1,200,000	Lumber
Standard	2x4	525	600	660	1,200,000	Grades
Utility		250	290	310	1,200,000	Authority
Select Structural		1550	1780	1940	1,500,000	(A Canadian
No. 1 & Appearance	2x5	1350	1550	1690	1,500,000	Agency)
No. 2	and	1100	1260	1375	1,400,000	
No. 3	Wider	650	750	810	1,200,000	
Stud		650	750	810	1,200,000	

Allowable Spans for Floor Joists

Joist Size (in.)	Spacing (in.)	Modulus of Elasticity, "E", in 1,000,000 psi									
		0.4	0.5	0.6	0.7	0.8	0.9	1.0	1.1	1.2	1.3
2 x 6	12.0	7-5	8-0	8-6	8-11	9-4	9-9	10-1	10-5	10-9	11-0
	13.7	7-1	7-8	8-2	8-7	8-11	9-4	9-8	10-0	10-3	10-6
	16.0	6-9	7-3	7-9	8-2	8-6	8-10	9-2	9-6	9-9	10-0
	19.2	6-4	6-10	7-3	7-8	8-0	8-4	8-8	8-11	9-2	9-5
	24.0	5-11	6-4	6-9	7-1	7-5	7-9	8-0	8-3	8-6	8-9
	32.0					6-9	7-0	7-3	7-6	7-9	7-11
2 x 8	12.0	9-10	10-7	11-3	11-10	12-4	12-10	13-4	13-9	14-2	14-6
	13.7	9-4	10-1	10-9	11-4	11-10	12-3	12-9	13-2	13-6	13-11
	16.0	8-11	9-7	10-2	10-9	11-3	11-8	12-1	12-6	12-10	13-2
	19.2	8-5	9-0	9-7	10-1	10-7	11-0	11-4	11-9	12-1	12-5
	24.0	7-9	8-5	8-11	9-4	9-10	10-2	10-7	10-11	11-3	11-6
	32.0					8-11	9-3	9-7	9-11	10-2	10-6
2 x 10	12.0	12-6	13-6	14-4	15-1	15-9	16-5	17-0	17-6	18-0	18-6
	13.7	11-11	12-11	13-8	14-5	15-1	15-8	16-3	16-9	17-3	17-9
	16.0	11-4	12-3	13-0	13-8	14-4	14-11	15-5	15-11	16-5	16-10
	19.2	10-8	11-6	12-3	12-11	13-6	14-0	14-6	15-0	15-5	15-10
	24.0	9-11	10-8	11-4	11-11	12-6	13-0	13-6	13-11	14-4	14-8
	32.0					11-4	11-10	12-3	12-8	13-0	13-4
2 x 12	12.0	15-2	16-5	17-5	18-4	19-2	19-11	20-8	21-4	21-11	22-6
	13.7	14-7	15-8	16-8	17-6	18-4	19-1	19-9	20-5	21-0	21-7
	16.0	13-10	14-11	15-10	16-8	17-5	18-1	18-9	19-4	19-11	20-6
	19.2	13-0	14-0	14-11	15-8	16-5	17-0	17-8	18-3	18-9	19-3
	24.0	12-1	13-0	13-10	14-7	15-2	15-10	16-5	16-11	17-5	17-11
	32.0					13-10	14-4	14-11	15-4	15-10	16-3

4 Use charts such as these to determine proper joist dimensions.

left side of the chart, then locate their spacing (in this example they are 16 inches on center). Follow the chart across until you find figures under the "E" column corresponding to 1,200,000. In this case, the maximum span for these joists is 9 feet 9 inches. If the joists span more than this they will not support a new bedroom in the attic.

The span table shown here is for sample purposes only and assumes live loads of 30 lbs/psf and dead loads of 10 lbs/psf. The appropriate chart for your project, however, depends on local codes, the species of wood generally used where you live, and the use of the room. If you find that the existing joists are undersized, correct this problem before proceeding with the attic conversion.

Reinforcing a Floor

Reinforcing a floor is not a complicated task but figuring out the right dimension of reinforcement can be. For this reason have a structural engineer specify the dimension, spacing and connection methods for reinforcement. There are several possibilities he or she might suggest. Note, however, that you cannot strengthen a joist simply by nailing additional wood on top of it.

Sistering a Joist. Reinforce an existing joist by sistering it to another equal-sized joist. One way to do this is to nail two-by lumber to one side of each existing joist. The new lumber must be as long as the existing joist so that it is supported in the same locations. Slip it into place atop the outer wall plate and cut a corner off one end to gain clearance beneath the roof.

Adding Joists. If the existing joists were closer together the floor would be stronger. Although you cannot readily move the joists you can add new ones. In effect this changes the joist spacing of the entire floor. If you do not want to sacrifice headroom in the attic by adding deeper joists, you may be able to add enough joists of the the same dimension as the old

Sistering a Joist. Reinforce an existing joist by attaching another equal-sized joist alongside it.

Adding Joists. Make the floor stronger by toenailing new joists to the wall plates.

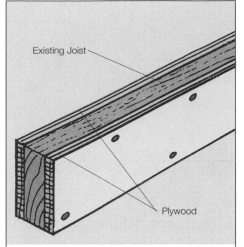

Joist Stiffeners. Plywood stiffens joists, thereby reducing the tendency of the floor to bounce.

ones. To determine whether or not this works for your situation check the joist span tables under several different joist spacings.

Joist Stiffeners. If the existing floor system is fairly strong but not stiff enough for the job, an engineer might recommend that you attach strips of plywood to each side of each joist. Plywood is only 8 feet long, however, so it will not span the same distance as the joist (hence, the reason it is useful for stiffening the system but not for strengthening it). Nail and glue the plywood to each joist.

Checking the Subflooring

The subfloor has two important roles: It stiffens the floor system and serves as a base for the finish floor. The proper grade and thickness of subflooring material depends on the spacing of the joists and the type of finish flooring to be installed. If subflooring is already in place in the attic make sure it is suitable. Subflooring made from 1x4 tongue-and-groove planks was common before plywood gained popularity. However, a planked attic floor usually is not flat enough to serve directly as a substrate for finished floor surfaces and probably is not thick enough to handle the live loads of a living space. Covering it with plywood will cost you some headroom, so in general it is

best to remove the planks and put them to use elsewhere.

Plywood Types. Plywood is perhaps the most commonly used product for the subfloor, though oriented strand board (OSB) also is used. The 4x8-foot size of these panel products covers large areas in a minimal amount of time and their surfaces are smooth enough for the direct application of some floor coverings (without a need for underlayment).

Use an interior-grade subflooring plywood that is thick enough to span between each joist without noticeably deflecting. Plywood is rated for joist spacings of 16 to 48 inches. The greater the spacing, the thicker the plywood. Note that the depth of a joist is not a factor; it is the spacing between the joists that is critical. Subflooring plywood also is graded by use. Panels suitable for use directly under carpeting and pad are in one category, while panels that require underlayment before the application of floor coverings (particularly vinyl) are in another category.

Finally, subflooring plywood is available in two edge configurations: square edge and tongue-and-groove edge. You can use either type of edge under any kind of flooring, but the cheapest, easiest choice depends on what you are planning for a finished floor.

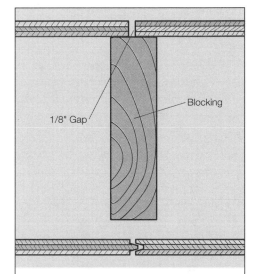

Plywood Types. Square-edged plywood (top) is more common and less expensive than tongue-and-groove plywood (bottom), which eliminates the need for blocking beneath the seams.

Square-edged plywood is a little easier to put down and usually cheaper than tongue-and-groove. However, unless you will be covering the plywood subfloor with underlayment that is at least 1/4-inch thick or wood strip flooring that is at least 3/4-inch thick, you'll be required to install blocking between the joists so that all edges are continually supported. With the underlayment, you must stagger the joints so they don't fall directly over the joists in the subfloor.

If you aren't planning a 3/4-inch-thick wooden floor over your subfloor, you'll probably find tongue-and-groove cheaper and more convenient. That's because the tongue-and-groove joint eliminates the need for blocking between joists even if you don't use underlayment or 3/4-inch-thick strip wood. As a result, tongue-and-groove boards designed to be used without underlayment is a great way to go if you are planning to use resilient flooring, tile, or carpet.

Installing Subflooring

Lay the subfloor far enough into the eaves so that it supports the knee walls that may be installed later. There is no need to run it all the way to the wall plates unless you plan to use the space behind the knee wall for storage. Subflooring material usually is nailed to the joists. For a stiffer floor that is less likely to squeak later on, run a bead of construction adhesive along the top of each joist just before nailing the plywood.

Note: *Sometimes the hammering that goes along with nailing causes fragile plaster ceilings below the attic to crack. It can also cause drywall nails to pop. To minimize the risk do not nail the subflooring material in place. Instead, use an electric variable-speed drill fitted with a Phillips screw tip to install the subfloor with drywall-type screws.*

Tongue-and-groove plywood is installed much in the same way as square-edged plywood. Manufacturers recommend a 1/8-inch expansion gap at joints. After nailing one row in place use a scrap of wood and a sledge to drive the adjacent row into position. It is best to orient sheets groove-side out because once one sheet has been nailed down it is easier to insert the tongue of the next sheet into a groove than vice versa.

1 Planning the Work. Always lay plywood with the best face up and the grain of each panel running at right angles to the joists. This makes the best use of the plywood's strength. Also, start every other row of plywood with a half-panel so that end joints will not run continuously along the floor. Make sure each edge of every sheet rests on a joist. Add blocking, if necessary, between joists. The ends of all panels must be centered on a joist.

2 Laying the Panels. Lay panels from the centerline of the floor towards the eaves so that you have a solid platform from which to work.

When laying a subfloor over joists that overlap a supporting wall install blocking between the overlaps. This supports one edge of the plywood. Offset adjacent sheets as needed so that edges fall over the joists.

3 Nailing the Panels. Manufacturers recommend that you allow a gap of 1/8 inch between square-edged panels to allow for expansion. You can gauge this distance easily by slipping a nail between panels as you position them. Nail two corners and then check the position of the sheet before nailing it down completely. Place nails at 6-inch intervals along edges of the sheet and at 10-inch intervals elsewhere.

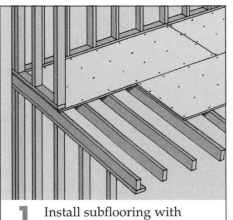

1 Install subflooring with staggered seams and the long dimension running across the joists.

2 To avoid back strain do not pick up the panel. Lift one edge and slide it into place.

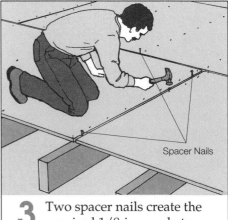

Spacer Nails

3 Two spacer nails create the required 1/8-in. gap between sheets. Place nails every 6 in. at the edges and every 10 in. in the field.

WIRING & PLUMBING

All attic conversions have to be wired for outlets and lighting, and if you are adding a home office you may need to accommodate other electrical appliances such as computers. Those building a master bedroom also face the challenges of adding plumbing fixtures.

Wiring the Attic

Whatever the scope of your project, it has to be wired and lighted. In some cases, such as building a home office, the electrical requirements may be considerable. Once you understand some of the basic concepts, wiring is not that difficult. It does require, however, that you pay stringent attention to safety and electrical codes. In some parts of the country only licensed electricians are allowed to work on household wiring while in other locales a homeowner may do all the work on his or her own. Be sure to check local codes before beginning work.

Adding Circuits

Though it is possible to extend an existing circuit to supply electricity to an attic with very modest needs, doing so may overload the circuit. Some codes, in fact, require that the renovated attic be equipped with new circuits. Not only are new circuits safer, they also make the attic far more convenient to use.

Service Entrance. Electricity enters the house through a meter which

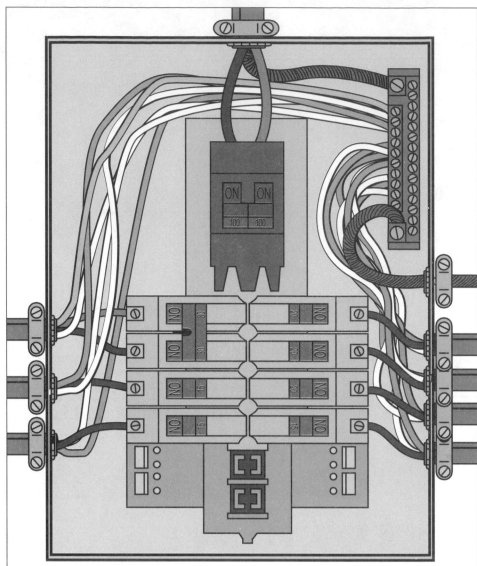

Service Entrance. Each incoming cable is connected to a separate circuit breaker. The panel shown here has room for four additional breakers so it can serve as many as four additional circuits.

Electrical Safety

■ Always turn off the power at the main electrical service panel before beginning work.

■ Always use tools that have insulated handles. Do not use screwdrivers that have metal shanks that extend completely through the handle. Even though the handle is insulated the exposed shank can transmit an electrical shock to your hand.

■ Never use a metal ladder when working with electricity. Use a wood or fiberglass ladder instead.

■ Always use a voltage tester to test a wire for the presence of electricity before you work on it (even if you switched off the circuit).

measures the amount of electricity used. It then enters the service entrance panel. The panel essentially is a distribution center that divides incoming electricity into various branch circuits that serve various portions of the house. Each circuit is protected by a fuse or a circuit breaker that cuts power to a circuit in the event of an overload or circuit fault. Each circuit is independent of the others so when power is cut to one, the others remain unaffected and continue to do their job.

Adding one or more circuits requires that you cut power to the service panel, add the circuit breakers, route

wire to the attic, and connect all the outlets and switches to the new circuit. If you are not familiar with this work turn it over to a licensed electrician. To save money, however, you can do the time-consuming task of routing the wiring. Just leave the connections to the electrician.

Tools & Materials

Virtually all wiring jobs can be accomplished using a small assortment of tools. If framing is exposed for the "rough" wiring (running wires and installing boxes) you probably need nothing more than a hammer and an electric drill that has a 5/8-inch bit for

Screwdrivers. You need a standard slot screwdriver and a Phillips screwdriver, each with a non-conducting handle.

Needlenose Pliers. This is the perfect tool for snipping a wire to length and then bending the end into a tight loop to go around terminal screws.

Wire Stripper. This tool has cutter holes with diameters to match various wire gauges. It easily strips off insulation without nicking the wire itself.

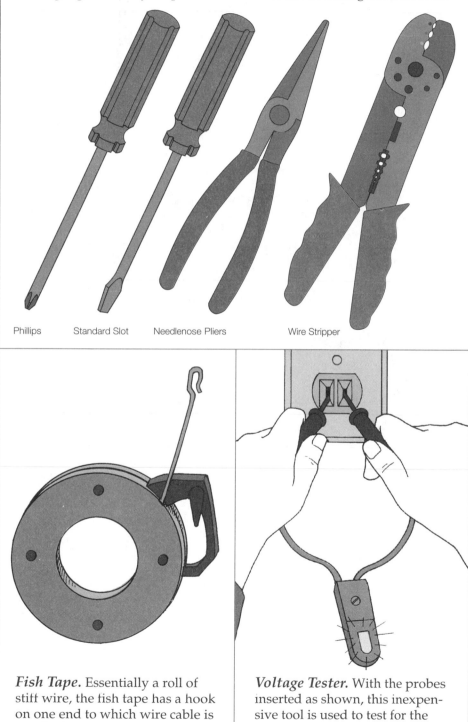

Phillips   Standard Slot   Needlenose Pliers   Wire Stripper

Fish Tape. Essentially a roll of stiff wire, the fish tape has a hook on one end to which wire cable is attached. The wire is then pulled through the wall.

Voltage Tester. With the probes inserted as shown, this inexpensive tool is used to test for the presence of electricity.

drilling through the studs. A fish tape is needed for running wire up to the attic through finished walls. The "finished" wiring work (installing switches, receptacles and fixtures) requires only a small collection of hand tools.

Running Wires

House circuits usually are wired with nonmetallic sheathed cable which is flexible, easy to work with, and often referred to by the trade name Romex. A cable is made up of two or more copper wires grouped together within a protective plastic sheathing and normally is sold in rolls of 25, 50 or 100 feet. Aluminum wire was used widely from World War II through the mid-1970s, but is no longer considered suitable for household wiring. Consult an electrician before modifying an aluminum wire system in any way.

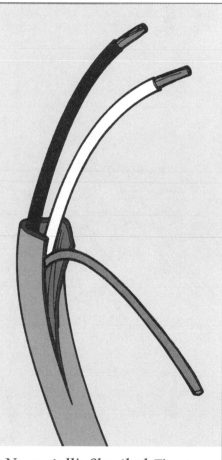

Nonmetallic Sheathed. The standard cable used for residential wiring has a sheathing of flexible plastic that protects several wires.

As it loops through the house, wiring is supported by heavy-duty cable staples that are driven into framing lumber with a hammer. Most attic projects require at least two boxes of staples. Make sure they are sized to the specific gauge of wire used.

Joining Wires

At one time all wires in a household system were spliced together with solder and electrical tape. Now splices are made by joining wires with plastic caps called wire connectors. The inner portion of each cap is threaded. To join two or more wires simply strip insulation from each wire, hold them together, and twist the wire connector in a clockwise direction. Connectors come in many sizes; choosing the right one depends on the number of wires to be joined and the gauge of the wires. Most often you will join two or three No. 14 or No. 12 wires. It is cost-effective to buy a box of wire connectors in the size most often needed rather than few at a time.

Have some plastic electrician's tape on hand. Electricians sometimes wrap a turn or two of tape around the base of a wire connector to ensure its staying power. Tape is useful for other general purposes as well.

Types of Cable

The individual wires (called conductors) in a cable are available in a range of diameters. These diameters are expressed in gauge numbers; the higher the gauge number the smaller the wire diameter. The more amperes a circuit is designed to carry, the larger the wire diameter requirement. Amperage is a measure of current flow. Circuits serving lighting and standard receptacles typically are 20 amps or 15 amps. Use 12 gauge wire for 20 amp circuits and 14 gauge for 15 amp circuits. Markings found on the plastic sheathing of cable explain what is inside and identify the type of insulation covering. For example, consider the following designation:

14/2 WITH GROUND, TYPE NM, 600V (UL).

The first number tells the size of the wire inside the cable (14 gauge). The second number tells you that there are two conductors in the cable. There also is an equipment grounding wire, as indicated. Each wire is wrapped in its own plastic insulating sheath, though the ground wire may be bare. In this case the type designation indicates a cable that is for use only in dry locations (in other words, indoors). Following the type is a number that indicates the maximum voltage allowed through the cable. Finally, the UL (Underwriters' Laboratories) notation assures you that the cable has been certified as safe for the uses for which it was designed. For safety reasons, never use wiring or other electrical supplies that do not bear the UL listing.

Estimating Wire Needs

New wiring that leads from the service panel to the first switch or outlet in the attic must be a continuous, unbroken length. The code allows certain exceptions to this rule, but a single length is ideal and almost always possible. You may have to snake wiring over, around, or through a number of obstructions en route to the attic, particularly if the service panel is in the basement. Rather than try to calculate the length of this path, begin with a 50-foot roll of wiring. In most cases, it is more than enough to reach from panel to attic. The excess, if any, can be used for general needs once the attic is reached.

When running wire through a structure in which all the walls are exposed, such as the attic itself, it is fairly easy to figure out how much you need. Measure the distance between each connection you have to make and add a foot for every connection. Total this amount and then add 20 percent to provide for a margin of error.

Getting Wire to the Attic

Getting wire from the service panel to the attic calls for considerable ingenuity. Every house requires a different

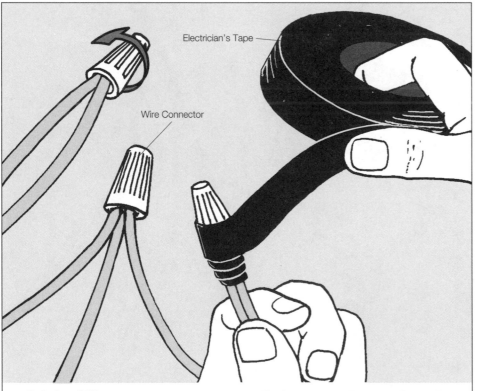

Joining Wires. Wire connectors are small plastic caps that join the ends of wires. Even though the caps should stay in place on their own, some electricians wrap the base with a turn or two of electrician's tape.

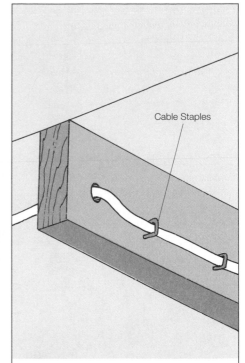

Securing Cable. Heavy metal staples are used to hold cable in place against the sides of joists. The staples are hammered in place but do not pinch the cable.

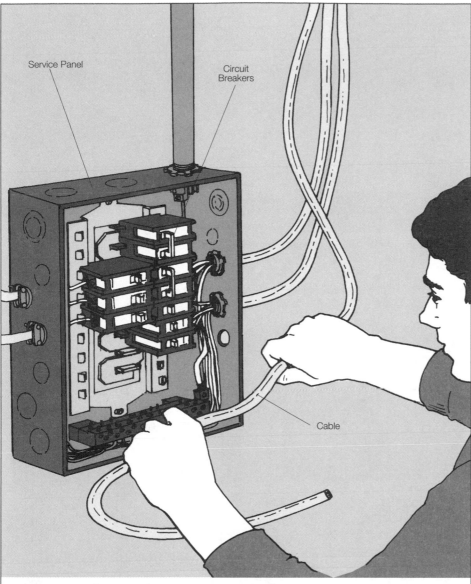

Wiring at the Panel. When stringing cable to new circuits leave an extra length near the box to connect it to the proper circuit breaker.

Drilling Through Framing. A nailing plate protects cable that passes close to the edge of a joist or stud. Barbs on the plate are pounded in with a hammer.

strategy, but the following guide provides some techniques for solving typical problems. Do not connect wires to a power source until they have been safely connected to outlets or fixtures.

Wiring at the Panel. Start the run with a 4-foot tail of wire at the service panel; this allows enough wire for the electrician to connect the circuit breaker.

Securing Cable. According to code you must use cable staples to support the cable. Be careful not to damage the outer casing of the wire as you drive the staple home.

Drilling Through Framing. Drill a 5/8-inch-diameter hole in places where cable must pass through the framing. Though you can use a spade bit to do this, an auger bit (available at many hardware and home supply stores) is easier and safer to use. The hole must be located at least 1¼ inches from the edge of the stud to minimize the risk that a paneling or drywall nail may contact the wire at some point. If for some reason the hole must be closer, the National Electrical Code requires that the wiring be protected with a steel plate.

Drilling Through Joists. When drilling through a joist always put the hole in the center one-third of the board. The joist will be weakened if you drill through the bottom third, and you may run into nails if you drill through the upper third. Avoid notching the bottom of a joist to create a path for wiring.

If direct access to the attic does not exist try to route wiring along forced-air ducts, through pipe chases, or even through voids between the framing and a masonry chimney. Plumbing waste vents always lead to the roof so look for a path along one of them that might lead to the attic. In some cases you may have to run wiring into the garage, up the inside of a garage wall, and then into the attic. Exposed wiring must be housed in rigid electrical conduit that is properly anchored to the wall. Check your local codes.

Using Fish Tape

If a clear path to the attic cannot be found you may have to run wire through existing interior walls. A fish tape is used to guide the wire through wall cavities.

1 Locating the Bottom Plate. From the basement, locate the underside of a wall through which you are going to run wire. Look for nails that penetrate the subfloor as a clue to the location of the wall. Wiring that disappears into a hole in the subfloor is another clue. You also can measure from an exterior wall, or from a landmark that is visible above and below the floor (a stairway or plumbing pipe, for example). Identify all doorways in the area. If you are running wire to the attic of a two-story house, make sure there is a second-story wall directly over the first story wall you have chosen.

2 Drilling an Access Hole. Once you have located the wall, drill a 1/4-inch pilot hole through the floor directly below the wall. Stick a length of coat hanger through the hole, securing it temporarily, and

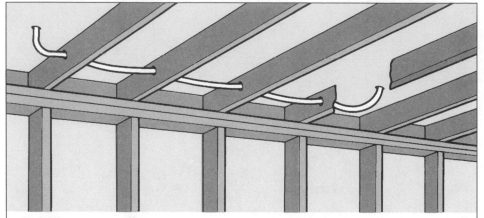

Drilling Through Joists. Use an auger bit and an electric drill to bore through joists. Holes are strategically located to minimize joist damage and keep the cable out of harm's way.

1 From the basement, look for the location of the wall you wish to run wire through by searching for clues, particularly other wires running through the floor.

then go upstairs. If you cannot see the coat hanger, you have drilled successfully into the interior of a wall. Go back and enlarge the hole using a 5/8-inch bit.

3 **Locating the Top Plate.** In the attic, locate the top plate of the same wall and drill a 5/8-inch hole

through it. The hole must be directly above the first hole.

4 **Make the Ceiling Notch.** If you working in a two-story house, you'll need to pull the wire through in two stages. The first stage is getting the wire from the basement to the first floor ceiling. To do this, make

a small cutout from the ceiling and wall juncture to expose the first floor top plate as shown. Notch the top plate so you can get the cable into the second-story wall.

5 **Fishing for the Wire.** For a one-story house, slide fish tape into the wall through the hole in the base-

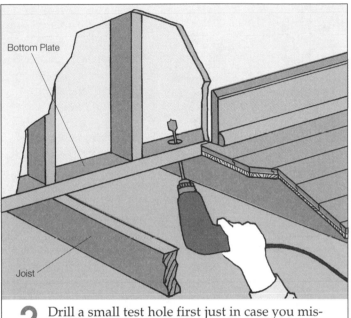

2 Drill a small test hole first just in case you misjudged the location of the wall (a small hole is easy to patch). Enlarge the hole when you are sure it is in the right place.

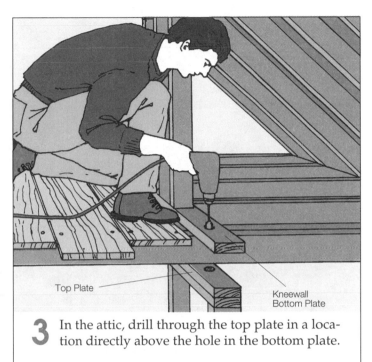

3 In the attic, drill through the top plate in a location directly above the hole in the bottom plate.

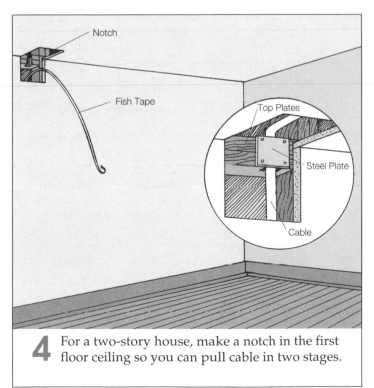

4 For a two-story house, make a notch in the first floor ceiling so you can pull cable in two stages.

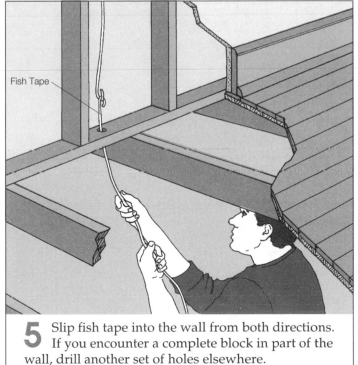

5 Slip fish tape into the wall from both directions. If you encounter a complete block in part of the wall, drill another set of holes elsewhere.

Fish Tape

Wires

Electrician's
Tape

Cable

Studs

Bottom
Plate

Joists

6 Pull the upper tape into the basement and tape cable to it. Make sure that nothing snags the other wires as you pull the cable through the wall.

ment and the hole in the attic and try to hook them together. This is not easy, particularly if there is wiring or pipes in the wall already. Have patience and you will succeed. For a two-story house, hook tapes from the basement to the ceiling notch.

6 **Attaching the Cable.** Pull the snagged upper tape into the

basement, attach the wire cable to it and tape them together. For a one story house, hoist the upper tape through both holes and into the attic as a helper feeds wire into the wall. For a two-story house, hoist the cable through the first floor ceiling notch. Disconnect the cable, hook fish tapes from the notch to the attic hole

and repeat the process to bring the cable into the attic. Cover the ceiling notch with a steel plate before patching the ceiling and wall.

Installing Plumbing

Plumbing is "roughed in" (pipes installed) before the subfloor is installed. This allows you to use the space between floor joists for piping if necessary. Run piping parallel to the floor joists wherever possible. It is best to locate a new bath above or close to an existing bath on the floor below because it provides easier access to plumbing supply lines and the drain, waste, vent (DWV) system. It also prevents plumbing noises from disturbing other living and sleeping areas. Adding plumbing supply lines is relatively easy for a homeowner to do, but tapping into existing DWV lines can be tricky. Unless you are familiar with plumbing codes and techniques consult a licensed plumber.

Assuming that there is enough space for the bathroom, the problems arise when tapping into the existing waste system. Waste lines can be difficult to position because they have to be sloped at least 1/4 inch per foot for proper drainage. This, and the 1½-inch diameter of the pipe, means that only relatively short waste lines fit between the joists.

Making Room for a Drain Line

If the drain line has to run a considerable distance perpendicular to the joists, you may have to build the new bathroom on a platform. A platform can add enough depth to the floor structure to accommodate unusually long drain lines. Check to make sure there is enough ceiling height to accommodate this strategy. Also, check local codes regarding the suitability of a bathroom raised by a step.

BUILDING ATTIC STAIRS

Designing and planning an attic stairway can be one of the toughest challenges in converting an attic to living space. Once the location of the stair has been decided, plan the work carefully to ensure the best results.

Planning the Stairs

Choosing the location for a stair (see page 14) is sometimes an exercise in compromise. Building the stair, on the other hand, calls for careful attention to details and must never be compromised. An improperly built stair is a serious safety hazard. If an existing stairway leads to the attic make sure it is safe enough to withstand frequent use. It may require remodeling or repair.

Calculating Rise & Run

Once the location for the stair has been determined you must calculate the rise of the stairs and the run of the treads and risers. Doing this now allows you to adjust the details somewhat in order to fit the stair into the existing space.

1 Figuring Total Rise. The vertical distance between the finished attic floor and the floor below is called the total rise and is key to stair construction. First measure the distance below the attic; that is, the distance between the ceiling and the floor. If the floor below the attic is carpeted measure to the subfloor beneath the carpet. Add to this figure the thickness of the existing ceiling and the actual depth of the attic joists. Then add the thickness of the attic subfloor to be installed and the thickness of

floor underlayment, if any. Finally, if the attic will have hardwood flooring add that thickness as well. The sum of these measurements is the total distance the stair rises from floor to floor. Let's say, for example, that the total rise is 102 inches.

2 Calculating Riser Height. Determine the number of steps that fit into the total rise and exactly how tall each one will measure by dividing the total rise by 7 inches (the ideal riser height as far as safety goes). Round down the figure to the nearest whole number. The result is the number of risers needed for the

stair. In our example, 102 inches divided by 7 inches is 14.57 inches. So we need 14 risers. Divide the total rise by the number of risers in order to get the exact height of each riser; this is called the unit rise. In our example 102 inches divided by 14 equals $7\frac{9}{32}$ inches.

3 Figuring the Run. The number of treads a stair has is always one less than the number of risers. The ideal width for a tread is about 11 inches.

Subtract the width of the nosing (an inch is common) to arrive at the "unit

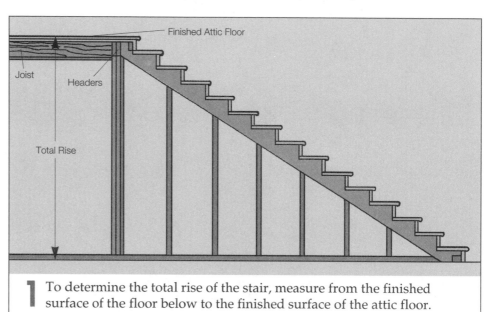

1 To determine the total rise of the stair, measure from the finished surface of the floor below to the finished surface of the attic floor.

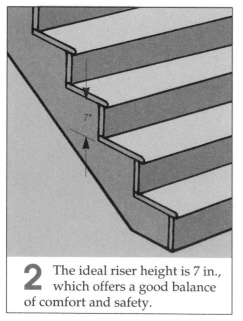

2 The ideal riser height is 7 in., which offers a good balance of comfort and safety.

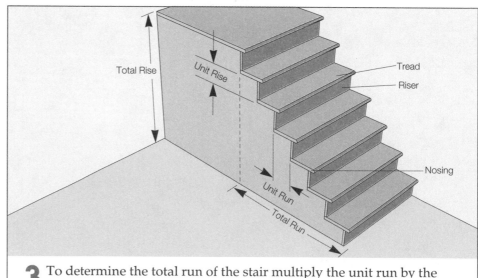

3 To determine the total run of the stair multiply the unit run by the number of treads. Note that the actual width of the final tread includes a nosing that usually is 1 in. wide.

Basic Stair Dimensions

Building codes are strict when it comes to stair construction. In part this is because small variations in details such as step height make a big difference in the safety of the stair. Check your local codes because they may differ from the guidelines noted below.

■ The width of the stair must be at least 36 inches. Measure between finished walls.

■ Nosings (if used) must not project more than 1½ inches.

■ Headroom must measure at least 6 feet 8 inches from the tip of the nosing to the nearest obstruction at all points on the stair.

■ Risers must be no more than 8¼ inches high.

■ Treads must be at least 9 inches wide.

■ All stairs made up of three or more risers must have a 30- to 38-inch handrail on at least one side. Handrails are measured vertically from the tip of the tread nosing. The end of the handrail must return to the wall or terminate in a newel post (this provides a clue to the end of the stairs even in the dark).

■ Landings must be the same width as the stair and at least as long as they are wide.

run" of each step, ideally 10 inches. With this figure it is easy to determine the total run of the stair (its overall length measured horizontally) simply by multiplying the unit run by the number of treads. In our example, the total run is 10 times 13 or 130 inches.

If your space for the total run is unlimited, your calculation is done. You can, however, play with the formula as long as you meet all the tread and riser criteria. Let's say you want to make the total run as short as possible. Then try calculating the stairs with the maximum allowable riser height of 8¼ inches: 102 inches total rise) divided by 8¼ inches equals 12 risers. That means you need 11 treads. To keep the tread width and riser height total to 18 inches, you will need treads that are 9¾ inches wide, including the nosing. So, subtracting the nosing, 8¾ inches times 11 treads gives you a total run of 96¼ inches.

Cutting an Opening

To create the stairwell you must make a hole in the floor framing. Though the rough opening can be made perpendicular to the attic floor joists, it is easier and there is less to cut if you position the opening parallel to them.

When determining the width of the rough opening remember to add the thickness of the finished wall covering. For instance, if the finished stair will be 36 inches wide and the stairwell will be finished with 1/2-inch drywall, the rough opening must be 37 inches wide. The length of the rough opening depends on several variables including the run of the stair. However, in order to provide the mandatory 6 feet 8 inches of headroom at all points on the stair, it must be at least 120 inches long.

Building Stairs

Once you know the run of the stairs, the dimensions of treads and risers, and the size of the rough opening, you are ready to build the stairs.

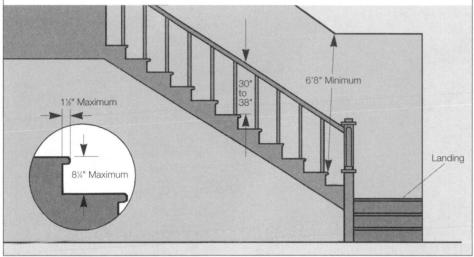

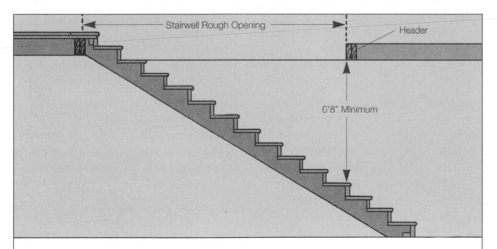

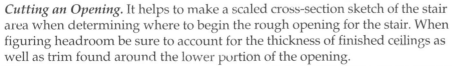

Cutting an Opening. It helps to make a scaled cross-section sketch of the stair area when determining where to begin the rough opening for the stair. When figuring headroom be sure to account for the thickness of finished ceilings as well as trim found around the lower portion of the opening.

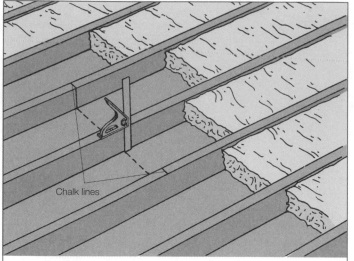

1 Mark the perimeter of the rough opening and snap chalk lines between these marks. Use a square to locate cutlines on the ceiling. Use tarps to cover the area below; then cut into the ceiling.

Chalk lines

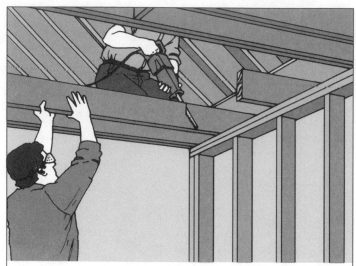

2 Have a helper support the joist as you cut it with a reciprocating saw. Shore up any long, unsupported joists with 2x4 bracing temporarily nailed to adjoining joists.

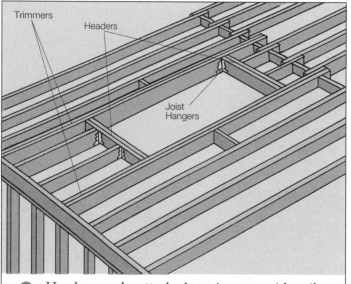

Trimmers

Headers

Joist Hangers

3 Headers can be attached to trimmers with nails or can be supported on joist hangers. Make sure trimmers are supported by a wall at each end.

Trimmer   Headers

Top Plate

Studs 16" on Center

4 The stairwell walls (if any) are built at this point. Nail the top plate to the underside of the trimmer joists and the bottom plate to the floor.

1 **Laying out the Rough Opening.** Remove all insulation from the area and relocate obstructions such as wiring or plumbing lines. Snap a chalkline across the tops of the joists to mark the rough opening. Using a square, extend the marks down to the attic side of the ceiling to locate where you will cut out the ceiling. Cut through the existing ceiling and remove it.

2 **Cutting the Joists.** In most cases at least two of the existing joists have to be cut in order to create the rough opening. Use 2x4 braces from below to temporarily support the joists on each end of the opening, then cut through the joists and remove them one by one. To prevent the wood from binding on the saw blade have a helper support each joist from below as you cut.

3 **Framing the Rough Opening.** Trimmer joists are the same dimension and length as the existing joists. They help carry the floor load instead of the joists you removed. Install the trimmers first, using 16d nails to attach them to the existing joists. Then support the headers and the ends of the cut joists with metal joist hangers.

4 **Framing the Stairwell.** If the stair will be enclosed build the walls now (see chapter 6) Stairs that are not enclosed must have a free-standing handrail system.

5 **Cutting Stair Stringers.** A stair is supported by three lengths of framing lumber called stringers. Use good quality 2x12 lumber that is straight and free from loose knots. Each stringer is cut with a series of identical notches to accommodate treads and risers. Use a carpenter's square to lay out the notches for the unit rise and unit run. Locate the dimension that corresponds to the unit rise (8 inches on the sample diagram). It is found on the outside edge of the square's tongue. Then locate the unit run. It is found on the

outside edge of the body of the square (10 inches on the sample diagram). Step off these dimensions along the stringer, then cut out the notches with a circular saw (do not overcut; use a hand saw to finish off the cut at each corner). Once you have cut one stringer use it as a template for laying out the others. Finally, trim off the top and bottom of each stringer.

6 **Adjusting the Stringers.** The height of the stringers must be adjusted to account for the thickness

of the treads. Otherwise the top step will be shorter than the others and the bottom step will be taller. This is called "dropping the stringers." Drop the stringers by the amount of one tread thickness by cutting this amount off the bottom of each stringer.

7 **Installing the Stringers.** A kicker made from 2x4 blocking helps keep the stair in position. Cut a notch in the bottom of each stringer to provide for it. Lift each stringer into place and make sure the treads are level. The outer stringers are spaced

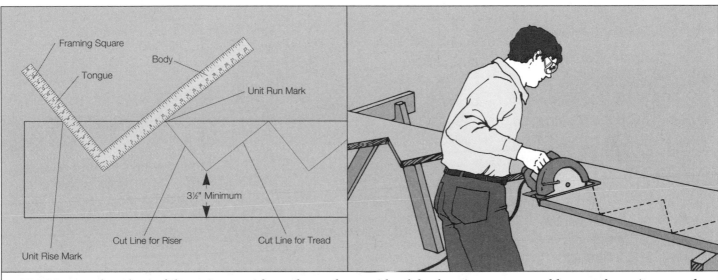

5 Line up the edges of the stringer with marks on the outside of the framing square and lay out the unit run and the unit rise of the steps onto the stringer (left). Use a circular saw to cut up to, but not through, the layout lines (right). Use a hand saw to finish up the cuts.

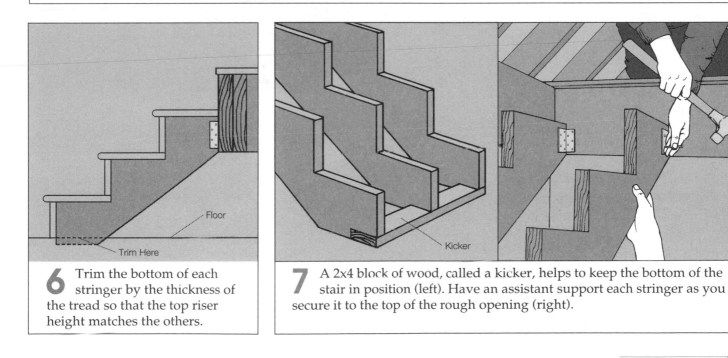

6 Trim the bottom of each stringer by the thickness of the tread so that the top riser height matches the others.

7 A 2x4 block of wood, called a kicker, helps to keep the bottom of the stair in position (left). Have an assistant support each stringer as you secure it to the top of the rough opening (right).

Treads

Stringers

Risers

Finishing Nails

Kicker

8 Fasten treads and risers with finishing nails. To minimize squeaks, put construction adhesive on the stringers before nailing on the treads and risers.

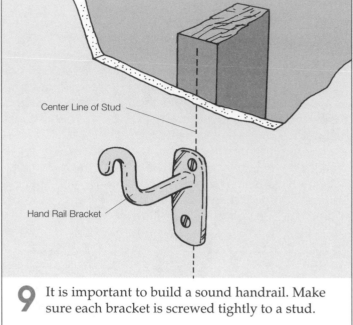

Center Line of Stud

Hand Rail Bracket

9 It is important to build a sound handrail. Make sure each bracket is screwed tightly to a stud.

1/2 inch away from the surrounding walls. This allows you to slip drywall into place rather than cutting it to match the stair angle. Use a metal framing anchor to secure the top of each stringer. Then toenail the bottom into the kicker and nail the kicker to the floor.

8 **Installing Treads and Risers.** If the stair will be carpeted use 1⅛-inch-thick plywood to make the treads; risers need only be 3/4-inch plywood. Use solid wood for a stair that will not be carpeted. If you planned earlier to include a nosing on each tread add its width to the unit run; the result is the actual width of the tread. Use a table saw to cut risers and treads to size and nail them to the stringers as you work your way up the stairs. Use nails and construction adhesive to attach the treads and risers.

9 **Securing the Handrail.** After the interior of the stairwell is finished with drywall, install at least one handrail along the entire length of the stair (including landings). The handrail must be 30 to 38 inches high. Locate the support brackets along a chalk line and screw each one into a stud. Then cut a handrail to length and attach it to the brackets.

Building a Platform Stair

If there is not enough space for a straight-run stair, a platform stair may solve access problems. This type of stair is made up of a pair of short, straight-run stairs that are supported by a platform (also called a landing). The platform is built as if it were an elevated section of floor (wood framing supports joists sheathed with a plywood subfloor). Pay particular attention to codes relating to the platform and the railing.

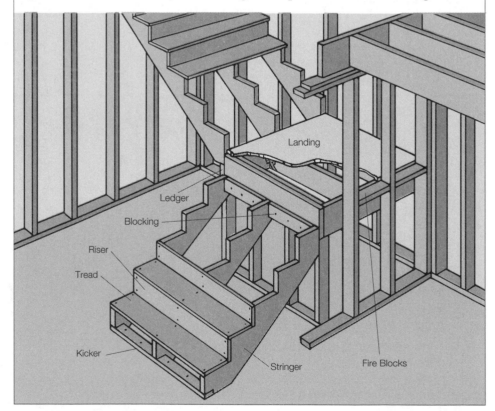

Landing

Ledger

Blocking

Riser

Tread

Kicker

Stringer

Fire Blocks

INSTALLING SKYLIGHTS & WINDOWS

It is rare for an unfinished attic to come equipped with enough natural light and ventilation for a comfortable, safe living space. Skylights and windows make a dramatic difference in a room and they are the essential tools for increasing natural light and ventilation.

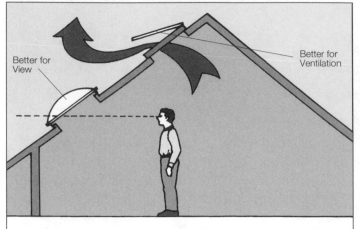

Better for View

Better for Ventilation

Determining Skylight Height. The location of a skylight not only affects your ability to reach it, it also determines the window's effectiveness at ventilating the attic.

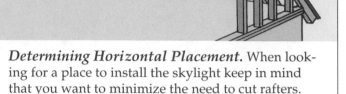

Determining Horizontal Placement. When looking for a place to install the skylight keep in mind that you want to minimize the need to cut rafters.

Installing Skylights

A skylight can be installed in a pitched roof. Some of the work involves cutting through and removing the roof covering. For this reason, the difficulty of the project depends partly on the type of roof covering on your house. Cutting into a roof covered with slate, tile, or metal is not something most homeowners are encouraged to attempt. These materials must be cut with specialized tools and a skylight installed within such a roof must be waterproofed with special flashing. If your roof is made of slate, tile, or metal, contact a roofing contractor for advice.

Another issue that affects the difficulty of the job is the size of the skylight. Small skylights that fit between existing rafters eliminate the need for special framing. To install larger skylights you have to remove part of at least one rafter, and then reinforce roof framing on either side of the roof opening. If you have to remove more than two rafters consult an engineer for help in determining the proper sizing for headers.

Choosing a Location

The right location for a skylight inevitably is a compromise between aesthetics, function and ease of installation. Check for nearby tree limbs that may fall or bob in the wind and damage the skylight (do not forget to consider small trees that may pose a problem in the years to come). Prune offending limbs before installing the skylight.

Determining Skylight Height. The higher up on a ceiling you place a skylight the better it ventilates the attic. Keep it at least 12 inches from the ridge to provide room for framing and flashing. Placing the skylight lower on the ceiling sacrifices some ventilation and privacy but may gain a view. Another argument for a somewhat lower placement is to make the skylight easy to reach since you may open and close a skylight frequently depending on the weather. Make sure that the skylight is not in the way of cabinetry or furnishings you plan to install.

Determining Horizontal Placement. First of all, you must determine the size of the rough opening required for the particular brand and size skylight you plan to use (the rough opening, sometimes abbreviated RO, is listed in the catalogs you'll use to select your skylight). The rough opening is measured between framing members. Decide approximately where you want the skylight, then adjust the position of the rough opening to the right or left to minimize the need to cut rafters.

Skylight Wells. As you consider different places for the skylight, determine how the skylight will be trimmed out in each instance. Unlike skylights that are installed elsewhere, attic units do not require much of a shaft.

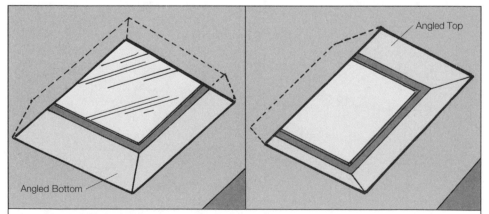

Angled Top

Angled Bottom

Skylight Wells. Though the sides of an attic skylight well are flat against the rafters, the bottom (left) or the top (right) or both can be angled to bounce additional light into the room.

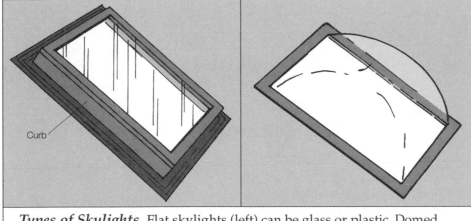

Types of Skylights. Flat skylights (left) can be glass or plastic. Domed skylights (right) are always made of plastic.

Ventilating. This unit opens to allow fresh air into the attic.

Instead, the opening beneath the skylight can be boxed off at right angles to the ceiling framing. One variation angles the upper or lower portion of the shaft (or both portions) outwards. This reflects more light into the room and is not difficult to do.

Types of Skylights

Skylights are glazed either with safety glass or plastic. A glass skylight is always flat while plastic skylights (acrylic or polycarbonate) usually are domed. In cold climates both types of glazing is best doubled (with an airspace in between) to minimize heat loss and reduce condensation problems. Glass is best tempered or wired to improve its strength and minimize danger if it breaks. Options include tinted glass to reduce glare, reflective glass to limit heat gain and frosted glass for privacy. You also can get low-E or argon-filled glazing from some manufacturers—if you live in a cold climate, it is a good idea to consider this option. An inefficient skylight contributes an uncomfortable chill to a room.

Ventilating. There are two basic types of skylights: ventilating and fixed. A ventilating skylight is hinged so it can be opened to allow air to flow. It usually has a screen and some sort of mechanism to prop it open. Large glass-glazed ventilating skylights sometimes are called roof windows.

Fixed. Fixed skylights cannot be opened and so they are less complex,

less expensive, and somewhat easier to install. If your attic conversion calls for more than one skylight consider using both types.

Curbed. Sometimes skylights are categorized by their method of installation. Many skylights rest on a wood frame called a curb that lifts the skylight above the plane of the roof. The curb usually is made of standard lumber and protected from the weather by metal flashing. Self-curb skylights are attached directly to the roof; no separate curb is necessary. These units sometimes are easier to install because they have integral flashing.

Installing a Curb-Type Skylight

To minimize the chance of damage from inclement weather, plan to complete the installation in one day.

Once the skylight is in place and tightly sealed the rest of the job can be completed from indoors at your convenience. Remember that the curb must fit the skylight and the roof opening must fit the curb, so check the layout instructions that come with the skylights before cutting into the roof.

The steps below are for a skylight installation that requires the removal of part of one rafter. If your skylight fits in between rafters the installation is similar but easier. You can use single headers instead of double headers unless manufacturer's installation instructions specify otherwise.

1 Locating the Roof Opening. Lay out the rough opening on the underside of the roof sheathing. Drive a nail through the sheathing (and the roofing) at each corner of the layout.

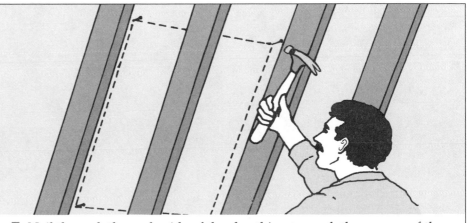

1 Nail through the underside of the sheathing to mark the corners of the cutout. Dotted lines show where the sheathing will be cut.

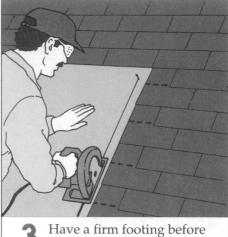

2 Use a spade to lift up roofing in the area to be cut. Be careful not to step on loose shingles; they are quite slippery.

3 Have a firm footing before cutting the sheathing with a circular saw.

The nails help locate the layout when you cut the sheathing from outside the attic. To strengthen the roof around a large skylight leave room for an extra rafter (called a trimmer) on each side.

2 Removing Shingles. Use an ordinary garden spade to pop up as many courses of shingles as necessary to clear the general area in which the skylight will be located. Remove all nails and use a utility knife to trim away the shingles and the underlying roofing felt from what will be the opening. The amount trimmed depends on the type of flashing used. Some curb-type skylights call for multiple courses of flashing, called step flashing, along the sides of the curb while others utilize a piece of flashing called a "collar" to keep out the water. When using step flashing trim the roofing about 2 inches away from the opening. If you are using one-piece flashing, trim enough roofing away so that the flashing rests directly on the sheathing. In either case, the goal is to remove as little roofing as possible.

3 Cutting the Roof Opening. Snap chalklines between the nails driven through the roof in step 1 to mark the portion of the sheathing to be removed. Use a circular saw set to a depth of approximately 3/4 inch (do not cut through rafters; they will be cut later). If the roof is pitched steeply it may be better to use a reciprocating saw from inside the attic. After the cut is complete, remove sawdust and debris from the roof to keep from slipping on it.

4 Cutting the Roof Framing. Use a square to mark cutlines along the sides of the rafter. The top and bottom cuts will be 3 inches outside the rough opening to provide room for doubled top and bottom headers. In order to pick up the roof load of the severed rafter, nail braces across several adjacent rafters and remove them only after the headers are in place. Use a circular saw to cut the rafter partway through. Then use a hand saw to finish the cut.

5 Installing New Framing. Slip the headers into place and use 16d nails for each connection through the rafters. Install a support rafter on either side of the rough opening and nail them to the existing rafters. In order to be effective the bottom of the support rafter must rest on the wall plate and its top must fit against the ridge.

4 Use an adjustable square to mark the cutlines on each rafter. Use a 2x4 or 2x6 to temporarily support rafters to be cut.

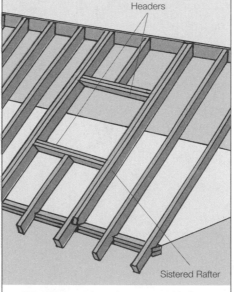

5 Use 16d nails to install the headers and to sister reinforcing rafters to each side of existing rafters.

6 Building the Curb. Consult the manufacturer's installation instructions and build the curb to the exact dimensions specified. The curb is a simple box made of 2x4s or 2x6s nailed together with butt joints and galvanized 12d nails. The inside dimensions of the curb are the same as the hole in the roof. Be sure the corners are square.

7 Installing the Curb. Bed the curb into roofing cement to provide an extra measure of water resistance. Nail the curb securely to the roof by toenailing it through the sheathing into the framing.

8 Sealing the Curb. With some skylights an angled strip of wood, called a cant strip, may be required in the places the curb intersects the roof sheathing. Bedded into roof cement and angled to shed water, it serves as an additional barrier against water infiltration.

9 Flashing the Curb. Whatever type of flashing you use, let it run at least 3 inches up the curb—the farther the better. Step flashing can be purchased at most building supply stores and actually is a system consisting of three elements: step flashing, head flashing, and base flashing.

Each L-shaped piece of step flashing overlaps the piece below and is installed to match shingle exposure. Install the base flashing first, then work your way up the roof slipping each piece of step flashing under a shingle. Once both sides of the curb are flashed, install the head flashing. Its top edge must slip under the closest row of shingles. Each flashing piece, except the head flashing, must be nailed through the top edge and into the curb. Dab a bit of roofing cement over nailheads to seal them.

10 Fastening the Skylight. First spread clear silicone sealant

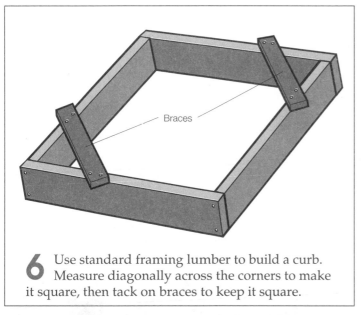

6 Use standard framing lumber to build a curb. Measure diagonally across the corners to make it square, then tack on braces to keep it square.

7 Set the curb in a bed of roofing cement and use galvanized nails to toenail it through the sheathing into the framing.

8 For additional waterproofing, seal the curb with cant strips and several coats of roof cement.

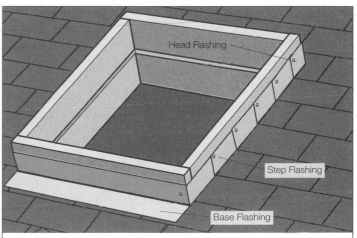

9 Step flashing consists of L-shaped pieces of metal that overlap to form a protective layer along the sides of the curb. Head flashing and base flashing protect the top and bottom of the curb.

10 Use sealant to seal the curb and press the skylight into place. Follow manufacturers instructions for fastening the skylight to the curb.

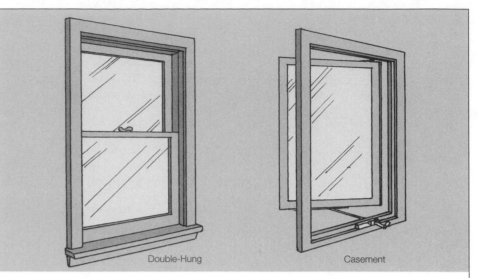

Types of Windows. Of the five basic types, double-hung and casement windows are the ones most commonly used for attic conversions.

Double-Hung

Casement

on the top edge of the curb and press the skylight into place. Use galvanized screws to secure the skylight to the curb. Check to see if your particular skylight can be secured from the inside to eliminate exposed fasteners.

Installing a Curbless Skylight

As far as laying out and cutting the rough opening goes, this installation is the same as that of a curb-type skylight. After that point, however, a curbless unit is much easier to install. There is no curb to build and

the flashing often is an integral part of the skylight itself.

1 Placing the Skylight. After the new framing is in place (step 5 of Installing a Curb-Type Skylight, page 48), place the skylight over the opening. Use roofing nails to secure just the top and side flanges to the sheathing—do not secure the bottom flange! Use mounting holes or special mounting brackets if the manufacturer provides them.

2 Completing the Installation. Extend the roof shingles over the

top and side flanges of the skylight, and under the bottom flange.

Installing Windows

Often an attic already has a window in one or both gable ends. It may be an operable unit originally intended for ventilation purposes or a fixed unit that simply allows a bit of light to penetrate. In either case it is most likely a single-glazed unit and not suitable for a living space.

Flange

1 Prepare the rough opening and set the skylight unit in place. Secure it with the hardware provided by the manufacturer. Use ladder hooks and roof jacks when working on a steep roof.

2 Replace shingles around the skylight to complete the installation. Do not nail through the bottom skylight flange.

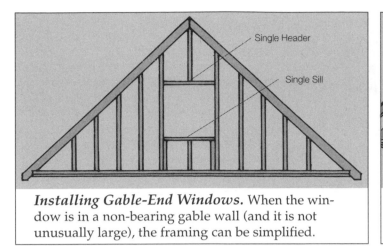

Installing Gable-End Windows. When the window is in a non-bearing gable wall (and it is not unusually large), the framing can be simplified.

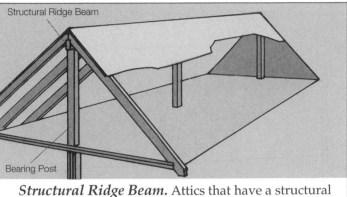

Structural Ridge Beam. Attics that have a structural ridge beam also have a bearing post in each gable end, so adding gable windows becomes more complicated.

Types of Windows

There are five common types of windows: sliding, fixed, awning, casement, and double-hung. Only casement and double-hung windows are appropriate for most attic projects. They can be used individually or combined in various ways to achieve dramatic effects.

Double-hung windows are perhaps the most common. They consist of two framed glass panels called sash that slide vertically and are guided by a metal or wood track. One variation, called a single-hung window, consists of a fixed upper sash and a sliding lower sash. The sash of some double-hung windows can be tilted inwards to make it easier to clean the outside. This is particularly handy for attics since windows are inaccessible from the outside.

Casement windows are hinged at the side and swing outward from the window opening when you turn a small crank. They can be opened almost completely for maximum ventilation. More importantly, they often are used as egress windows because most of the sash area is unobstructed when the window is opened.

Installing Gable-End Windows

With the exception of skylights and dormer windows, (see Chapter 7 Building Dormers) attic windows are installed in gable ends. It is easier to install windows in gable ends than it is to install them in other parts of the house. That is because the framing at

the gable ends rarely is load-bearing; all the load is carried by the rafters. If windows already exist in the gable end the framing around them probably is lighter than that found in the outside walls below. Instead of a heavy structural header often a single or double plate frames the top of the window. If this is your situation, you have complete flexibility in changing the framing to suit your window plan. Also, there is no need to provide temporary support for the wall while the framing is changed. The only thing that adds difficulty to working on gable-end windows is the fact that you are working high above the ground.

Structural Ridge Beams. If the attic has a structural ridge beam there is a possibility that the gable end is load bearing. In this case the ridge beam supports the top end of each rafter (rather than the other way around). The ridge beam, in turn, is supported by posts that run straight down the middle of each gable end. Structural ridge beams most often are used for cathedral-style ceilings because they eliminate the need for joists to keep the rafters from spreading. One clue to this situation is a ridge beam that is unusually heavy, such as built up 2x10s or a glue-laminated beam. Also, the rafters may be notched to sit on top of the beam instead of simply being nailed to the beam. If you think you may have a structural ridge beam consult a structural engineer, architect, or master framing carpenter before disturbing the gable end framing.

Framing the Window

All windows fit within an opening in the wall framing called a rough opening. The rough opening is slightly bigger than the overall dimensions of the window (measured at the jambs). The extra space allows the window to be plumbed and leveled as needed. The exact width and height of the rough opening is specific to the particular window you buy. It usually is best to wait until you have the window on hand before making the opening. The following procedure assumes the wall is not load bearing and there is no existing window in the gable end, however, the procedure essentially is the same for enlarging a window opening.

1 **Removing Studs.** Start by removing all the studs that cross

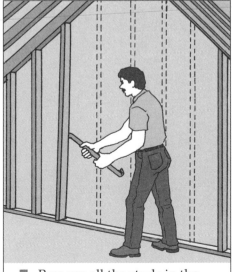

1 Remove all the studs in the area of the new window.

2 Install the studs that form the sides of the rough opening.

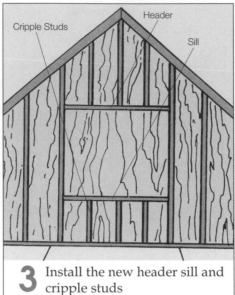

Cripple Studs   Header   Sill

3 Install the new header sill and cripple studs

4 Tack-nail a board to the siding. It acts as a guide as you cut the new window opening.

the area to be occupied by the rough opening. The studs meet the end rafter with angle cuts. In most cases one nail is toenailed through each stud into a rafter. Use a cat's paw to remove this nail. Next, release the studs from the nails coming through the bottom plate. There are two ways to do this: If you have a reciprocating saw, fit it with a metal cutting blade and cut in the places that the studs meet the plate, severing the nails. If you do not have a reciprocating saw use a hand saw to cut through the studs about 4 inches from the plate. The sheathing and the siding is nailed from the outside into the studs. Use a crowbar to pry the studs away from

these nails. Save the studs; they can be used for framing the new rough opening. If you used a hand saw to cut the studs, knock the remaining pieces free of the plate nails, then use a hacksaw to cut the protruding nails flush. Cut the nails that protrude through the sheathing as well.

2 **Installing Studs.** Lay out the width of the new rough opening on the sole plate. Use a long level or a plumb bob to transfer the width to the bottom of the end rafters. Measure each top and bottom mark to get the lengths of the studs for the new rough opening. The studs probably can be cut from studs that have been removed and they already have the proper angled cut on the top ends. Toenail these studs to the sole plate and rafters. Check for plumb.

3 **Installing Header, Sill, and Cripple Studs.** Cut the header and rough windowsill to fit between the designated studs. Attach them by nailing through the studs. If there is not enough room to swing the hammer, toenail the header and sill to the studs. The cripple studs are the short vertical members below the sill and above the header. In a nonstructural wall their only purpose is to provide nailing for drywall inside and sheathing and siding outside. Space the cripple studs as needed for nailing.

4 **Cutting the Opening.** From inside, drill a hole at each corner of the opening. Then go outside and snap chalklines to delineate the opening. All nails that are crossed by the line must be removed. If the siding is clapboard you must provide a level surface upon which the circular saw can ride by tacking a one-by board along the cutline as shown. Set the saw to cut through the siding and sheathing. Wear goggles or safety glasses and cut the opening.

Installing the Window

Windows are installed several ways. Some windows are installed by driving nails through the jambs and into the sides of the rough opening. These windows have a narrow casing (called brickmold) on the outside. Metal, vinyl and clad-wood windows usually are nailed to the sheathing through a perforated flange that surrounds the window (see Installing Flanged Windows, page 54). With this system you have to cut back the siding (but not the sheathing) to make room for the flange. You also need a window casing (used to cover the flanges). In another system the windows come with a heavier out-side casing that gets nailed to the outside of the rough framing and you have to cut back the sheathing as well as the siding.

The following directions pertain to the type of window that gets nailed through the jambs.

1 **Putting the Window in Place.** Unpack the window and check it for square by measuring the window jambs corner to corner. The diagonal measurements must match. If there are any braces or reinforcing blocks on the window leave them in place until the window has been nailed securely to the house. Some manufacturers recommend that the sash be removed before the window is installed to prevent glass breakage, while others recommend leaving the sash in place to stiffen the jambs. If the manufacturer permits, remove both sash to make the window easier to carry up the ladder. Lift the window

1 Wood windows are primed before they are installed. Remove the sash before installing the window. It is easier to lift that way.

2 Have an assistant shim the window while you check it for level from outside. Be sure the window is flat against the outside of the house.

into the rough opening and hold it there firmly as an assistant helps from the inside.

2 **Leveling the Window.** Check the sill for level. Shim beneath each jamb leg as needed. If the window is unusually wide, shim the sill midway between legs as well. Check the sill frequently throughout the installation to ensure that it has not shifted out of position. Tip the window away from the opening just enough for the person inside to run a bead of exterior-grade caulk behind the brickmold, then press the window against the wall.

3 **Setting the Window.** Use a 10d galvanized casing nail to nail through the casing, securing one lower corner of the window to the wall. A casing nail is similar to a finish nail but its shank is heavier than a finish nail of the same length. Insert flashing over the head casing and slip it beneath the siding. If flashing did not come with the window it can be purchased at a building supply store.

4 **Plumbing the Window.** Check the window for plumb; this is particularly important if you removed the sash earlier. Check the window again for square. If necessary, adjust it by slipping shims between the jamb and the framing. When the window is plumb use another nail to tack it in place.

Siding

Flashing

Head Casing

3 Do not set the nails completely until the window has been fully installed. Flashing is slipped beneath the siding and over the head casing.

4 Plumb and shim the jamb from inside the attic as needed. Check the window for square as well.

5 Nailing the Window. Install the sash and open and close them a few times. If they work properly, complete the nailing. If the sash bind, however, the window may have to be repositioned.

6 Sealing the Window. Use a high quality exterior caulk to caulk the gap between the window casing and the siding (do not forget to caulk beneath the sill). From the attic side of the window, use a fiberglass or foam sealant to seal the gap between the jambs and the rough opening. When using foam, spray it gradually to prevent it from pushing the jambs out of position. The window is now ready for the installation of interior casing.

5 Install the sash. If they fit properly and slide smoothly, finish nailing the window into place.

6 Use a high quality caulk to seal around the outer edges of the window (except at the head flashing) (left). Use fiberglass insulation or expanding foam sealant to seal gaps on the inside. (right).

Installing Flanged Windows

Flange

Many windows, including aluminum, vinyl and clad windows, have a perimeter nailing flange that makes installation easy. Rough openings typically are smaller than they would be for a standard window of the same size because there is no need to shim the sides of the window.

To secure a flanged window simply nail through the flange and into the framing of the rough opening (consult the window manufacturer's instruction sheet for the number and type of nails to use). Check the sill for level and shim beneath from inside the house as necessary. Begin nailing the window into place on one side using 1¾-inch galvanized roofing nails at least every 10 inches through the slots in the flange.

Continue nailing around the window, checking for plumb periodically as you go. The best technique is to drive the first few nails partway, fully driving them home only after checking again for plumb and level. Then install the trim or replace the siding around the window to match other windows in the house. The casing must fit snugly between the edges of the siding and the side of the window. Caulk in both places.

BUILDING DORMERS

Although building a dormer may seem like a small project it actually calls for a diverse collection of construction skills. In fact, building a dormer requires many of the same skills necessary to build an entire house. Still, building a dormer or two is well worth the effort for those who desire additional natural light, ventilation and a way to make the most of existing floor space.

Types of Dormers

Dormers change the roofline of the house and provide headroom where it is needed most (at the eaves). Because they are visible outside of the house you will want the dormers to be compatible with the style of the house. Use the same roofing, siding and window type and style used on the rest of the house. There are three basic types of dormers: gable dormers (sometimes called doghouse dormers), shed dormers and eyebrow dormers.

Gable Dormers. A gable dormer has a roof with two pitched planes that meet at a ridge, and usually a ceiling that is vaulted. The roof pitch need not match that of the house, though it may help the dormer fit in visually. A valley is formed at the intersection of the dormer roof and the surrounding roof to channel away water. Although a gable dormer is good for creating natural light and ventilation, its proportions restrict its size, making it ineffective when it comes to increasing usable floor space.

Shed Dormers. The hallmark of a shed dormer is its single, flat roof which is pitched at less of an angle than that of the surrounding roof. This type of roof is easier to build than the roof on a gable dormer. It also is easier to join to the existing roof because shingles simply lap over the inter-

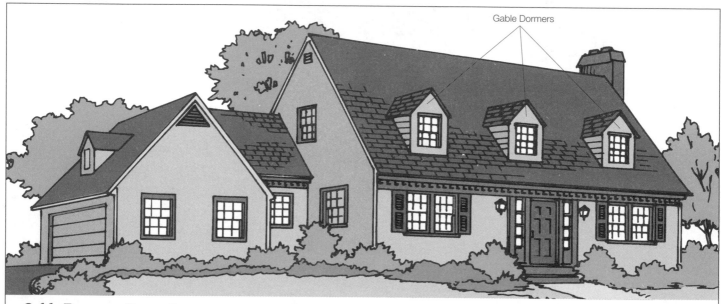

Gable Dormers. Depending on its size, a gable dormer accommodates one or more windows. The shape of the dormer ties it visually to the house.

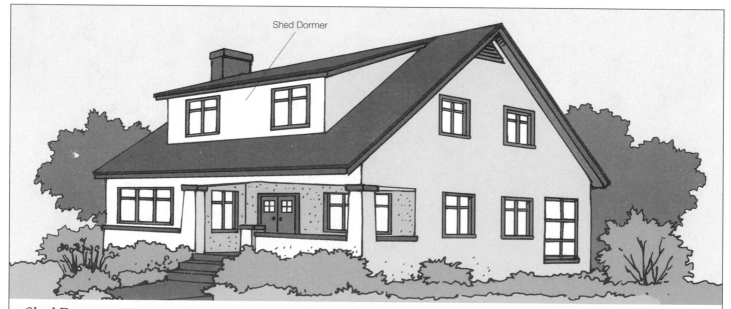

Shed Dormers. These usually are larger than gable dormers and are very effective at expanding the amount of usable floor space in an attic. A shed dormer can be small enough to house a single window or as long as the entire house.

Eyebrow Dormers. These small dormers sometimes are used strictly as architectural accents, but they can provide light and ventilation as well.

section. The ceiling inside a shed dormer either follows the upward slope of the rafters or is totally flat. The best feature of a shed dormer, however, is that it dramatically increases the usable floor space in an attic. Some shed dormers even run the length of the house, though the magnitude of such a project generally calls for a builder or structural engineer. As an option, you may want to add shed dormers on both sides of the roof; an arrangement that resembles saddlebags.

Eyebrow Dormers. Unlike other types of dormers, an eyebrow is used primarily to allow natural light into an attic or to serve as a decorative accent for certain house styles. Its small size and curved shape encourage the use of a fixed, rather than operable window. The window itself usually is custom-made but some manufacturers offer a limited selection of stock units.

Other Types of Dormers

Sometimes the outer wall of a gable or shed dormer is built in the same plane as the outer wall of the house. The house siding may continue up the face of the gable, or it may be interrupted by a small section of roof supported by short lengths of rafters called stubs or dummies. A dormer designed in this way gains the maximum amount of attic floor space and simplifies framing somewhat, but does not always fit in with the style of the house.

Other Types of Dormers. Flush dormers are in line with the front wall of the house. A flush shed dormer dramatically expands the living space (top). A flush gable dormer allows the window to be installed almost as low as the attic floor (middle). To maximize the size of window, tuck the dormer into the roof (bottom).

Another option is to recess the dormer into the roofline. Waterproofing in this case is quite a challenge so plan to do the work under the guidance of a builder and a roofer. A recessed dormer usually is found on houses that have a covered front porch.

Designing the Dormer

There are several things to consider when deciding upon the size and style of your dormer. For one, the dormer must be built in proportion to the house; a king-size dormer on a small roof causes the house to appear top-heavy, while a dormer that is too small does not admit a worthwhile amount of light. Take a drive around town and observe the various dormers. When you see one that you like note its size in comparison to the house.

Many people end up sizing the dormer to accommodate a particular window size, particularly if it complements other windows in the house. If this is the case the dormer must be at least 6 inches wider on each side than the rough opening of the window. Doing this provides strength at the corners of the dormer and accommodates framing details. Check local codes; the dormer window may have to be large enough to serve as an emergency exit (called an egress window).

Drawing a Section View

Before you cut a hole in the roof some careful planning is in order. Draw a section view (cross section or side view) of the existing attic framing. Then experiment with various dormer designs.

1 **Measuring the Pitch.** The pitch (angle) of a roof traditionally is expressed as the number of inches it "rises" for every foot it "runs." Rise is measured vertically while run is measured horizontally. Use a level and tape measure to figure pitch. Mark the level at a point 12 inches from one end, then hold the level against the underside of a rafter

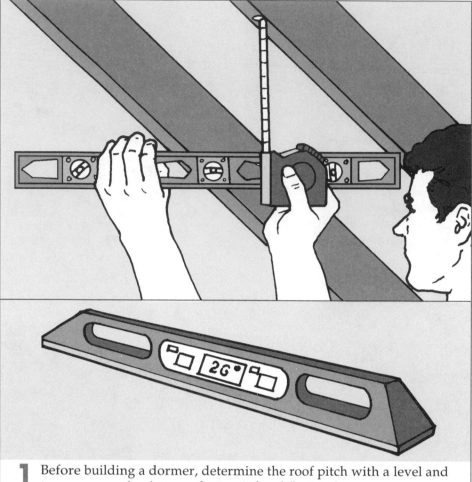

1 Before building a dormer, determine the roof pitch with a level and tape measure (top) or an electronic level (bottom).

until it reads level. Use the tape to measure the distance from the level to the rafter at the 12-inch mark. For example, if the distance from the rafter to the level is 11 inches, the rise is 11 inches in 12 inches of run. This is written as 11/12. Carpenters often express it as "11 in 12."

Another way to measure pitch is to place an electronic level, which provides a direct readout of roof pitch, against the underside of a rafter.

2 **Drawing a Cross Section.** Measure the width of the gable end, the outdoor height of its walls, the depth of the rafters and the depth of the attic floor joists. Use this information, along with the pitch of the roof (found in step 1), to draw a cross section of the house to scale. Be sure to include the ridge.

3 **Designing the Dormer.** Now that you have a cross section of the

house you can experiment with the size and placement of the dormer. (This example shows a shed dormer but drawing a gable dormer is much the same except that you might want to draw a front view as well.) Place a sheet of tracing paper over the drawing made in step 2 (or make photocopies of it) so you can make several dormer sketches without redrawing the house. Sketch a rafter first and then experiment with various locations for the dormer's face wall. In order for a shingle roof to drain properly rafters must have a pitch of at least 3/12 inches. They can extend all the way to the ridge if necessary. Measure from the attic floor to the underside of the dormer rafter to determine the headroom that results. Add details such as the header and plate for the window; this essentially is a cross-section view of the window's rough opening (include

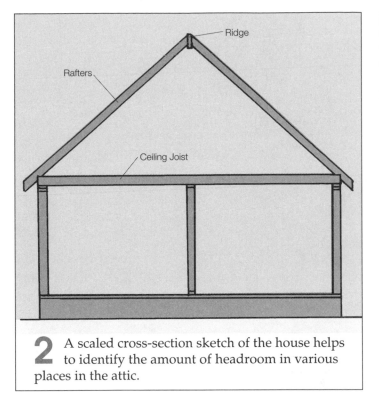

2 A scaled cross-section sketch of the house helps to identify the amount of headroom in various places in the attic.

Labels in image: Ridge, Rafters, Ceiling Joist

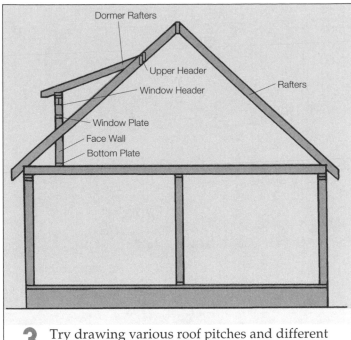

3 Try drawing various roof pitches and different locations and heights for the face wall. Ask an engineer if the ceiling joists can support the dormer.

Labels in image: Dormer Rafters, Upper Header, Window Header, Rafters, Window Plate, Face Wall, Bottom Plate

at least a double 2x6 header). The bottom of the rough opening must be at least 6 inches above the plane of the roof to allow room for flashing and window trim.

Once the construction details of the dormer are worked out you might want to see how it is going to look on your house. One way to do this is to make a scale drawing of the front of the house, and then draw in the dormer, along with its windows. Another way is to take a photo of the house and use a permanent marker to draw the dormer on it. Take a photo that includes both the front and one gable end of the house (a 3/4 view), allowing you to sketch in both the front and the side of the dormer.

Building Dormers

Although much of the construction is done from inside the attic, building a dormer requires that you spend a lot of time on the main roof. This is hazardous work. To minimize the risk of injury and to help the work proceed smoothly, be sure to have a stable working platform. A good extension ladder is your best asset.

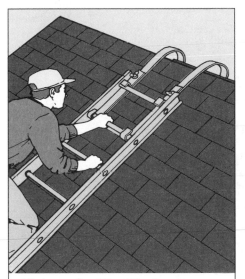

Using a Ladder Hook. This arrangement offers a secure grip and allows you to climb up and down the roof without stepping on shingles.

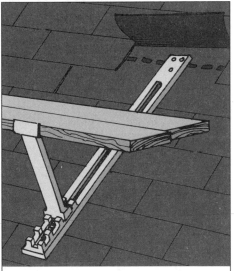

Using Roof Jacks. Pairs of adjustable metal brackets support a plank. Brackets must be nailed through sheathing into rafters.

Consider using a ladder hook or roof jacks (they can be rented if you do not own them).

Using a Ladder Hook. This handy device attaches to the top rung of a straight ladder and hooks over the ridge of the roof. It allows you to clamber up and down the roof with-

out damaging the shingles and is easily moved from location to location. As you work, it sometimes helps to place a ladder with a ladder hook on each side of the proposed dormer.

Using Roof Jacks. These metal brackets are used in pairs to support a wood plank; some even adjust to

1 Install plywood subflooring throughout the attic before beginning work on the dormer.

2 Locate the position of the face wall and the upper header on the subfloor. Both are parallel to the eaves of the house.

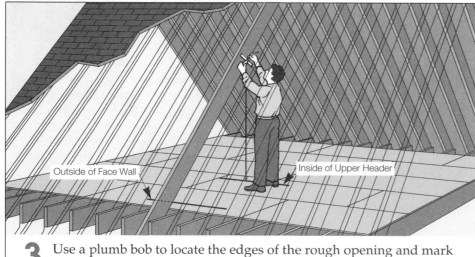

Outside of Face Wall

Inside of Upper Header

3 Use a plumb bob to locate the edges of the rough opening and mark these locations on the rafters. Hammer a small nail through the sheathing to mark the location of each corner.

the pitch of the roof. To install a jack, lift one shingle and nail the jack through the shingle below into roof framing. After you remove the jack, the nail holes will be covered by the shingle.

Building a Shed Dormer

In order to build a dormer you have to cut a large opening in the existing roof, so be sure to have all the necessary tools and materials (including windows) on hand before you start. This minimizes the amount of time that the house is vulnerable to changes in the weather. Purchase a heavy-duty waterproof tarp to cover the opening overnight or in the event of unexpected rain. Once the dormer is tight to the weather, the inside can be finished. Use fiberglass batts to insulate the walls and ceiling but do not block airflow above the ceiling insulation.

1 Installing the Subflooring. If you have not done so already, install plywood subflooring throughout the attic. Not only does this provide a safe platform from which to build the dormer, it also keeps demolition debris out of the floor joist cavities (and the insulation, if any). The subfloor must be in place to support the face wall of the dormer.

2 Locating the Opening. A shed dormer is built within the confines of a large rectangular hole cut into the roof. Essentially this hole is the rough opening for the dormer. Properly locating the rough opening on the sloping underside of the roof is important. First identify the rafters to be removed and then use dimensions taken from the cross-section drawing to snap two chalklines on the attic floor. One line represents the outside of the face wall and the other represents the inside face of the upper header.

3 Marking the Opening. Use a plumb bob to determine the points at which the chalked layout lines "intersect" the two rafters (called trimmers) that form the outside of the rough opening. Draw a plumb layout line on the rafters at each intersection, then drive a nail clear through the roof where the layout meets the underside of the roof sheathing. The nails appear on the roof, marking the corners of the opening.

4 Stripping the Roof. After securing the appropriate roof jacks or ladders, snap chalklines between the protruding nails. Then pound each nail back through the roof to keep from tripping on it later. Use a razor knife to score shingles along the chalked lines, then remove all shingles and roofing paper between the lines. Use a pry bar or flat spade to pry up the shingles. Spread a tarp over the plants and ground below to prevent nails and such from falling on the lawn.

5 Removing the Sheathing. Though this job can be done with a reciprocating saw from inside the attic (see Framing Variations, page 66), it generally is easier to cut with a circular saw while you are on the roof (especially on modestly-sloped roofs). Set the circular saw to a depth that just cuts through the sheathing (plywood sheathing usually is 1/2 inch thick; board sheathing usually is 3/4 inch thick). Use a carbide-tipped saw blade designed for demolition work to cut along all four sides of the rough opening. Then, from inside the attic use a hammer and pry bar to remove the sheathing (pull it into the attic instead of letting it fall from the roof).

(see Framing Variations, page 66)

4 Strip roofing from the general area in which the dormer will go. Do not damage more shingles than necessary. Clear away debris as you work to avoid slipping on it.

5 Set a circular saw to the thickness of the sheathing (this prevents you from cutting into the rafters). Make the top cut first and lean on the sheathing only while making this cut. Make subsequent cuts from the roof or the safety plank.

Setting up a Ladder

Follow these simple guidelines to increase your safety while working on and around extension ladders. Most of these tips apply to other types of ladders as well.

■ Always place the ladder on a firm, level surface. Many ladders can be fitted with nonslip feet that adjust to varying terrain.

■ Always face the ladder when climbing up or down.

■ Always keep your weight centered between side rails. Rather than dangerously overreaching and unbalancing the ladder, be sure to place the ladder where you need it.

■ Never use a bent or damaged ladder. If the ladder is damaged, replace it.

■ Follow the manufacturer's instructions for proper orientation of the extension; not all extension ladders work the same way.

■ Angle the ladder so that the distance at the bottom is approximately one fourth the height of the ladder.

■ Always extend the ladder far enough above the roof edge to provide something to hang on to as you board or leave the ladder.

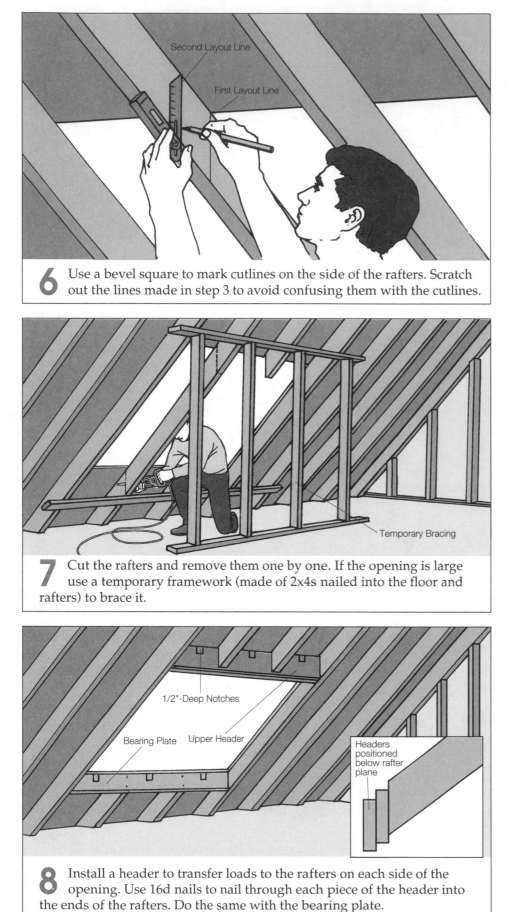

6 Use a bevel square to mark cutlines on the side of the rafters. Scratch out the lines made in step 3 to avoid confusing them with the cutlines.

7 Cut the rafters and remove them one by one. If the opening is large use a temporary framework (made of 2x4s nailed into the floor and rafters) to brace it.

8 Install a header to transfer loads to the rafters on each side of the opening. Use 16d nails to nail through each piece of the header into the ends of the rafters. Do the same with the bearing plate.

6 **Marking the Rafters.** Most of the remaining work can be done from inside the attic. At the top of the roof opening, mark each trimmer rafter with a second layout line 3 inches from the first (3 inches is the thickness of the header). At the bottom of the roof opening, draw additional layout lines but make them 1 1/2 inches from the ones drawn in step 3. Check all lines for plumb.

7 **Cutting the Rafters.** Before you begin cutting, support the rafters with temporary braces. Use a cross-cut hand saw or a reciprocating saw to cut one rafter at a time. Make your cuts at the second layout lines to make room for the header above and a "bearing plate," a type of sill you will install at the bottom of the opening. Make the bottom cut first, then have a helper support the rafter as you make the top cut to prevent the wood from binding on the saw.

8 **Installing the Headers.** Cut three pieces of lumber to fit between the trimmer rafters. This lumber must be the same dimension as the existing rafters (usually 2x8 or 2x10). At the bottom of the opening fit one of the pieces against the cut ends of the lower rafters, nail it in place and then nail the rafter ends to it. This bearing plate rests against the face wall of the dormer.

The two remaining pieces of lumber become the header at the top of the opening. Before installing the header pieces cut some shallow notches in the top edges (two notches in each bay will suffice). The notches allow air to circulate from the soffit vents into the rafter bays above (see chapter 6). Hold up one piece of lumber and nail it in place, then nail through it into the cut ends of the rafters. Slip the second piece into position and nail it in place, then nail through it into the first piece. It is okay that the two pieces are offset slightly due to the pitch of the roof.

9 **Doubling the Trimmer Rafters.** Each trimmer must be strengthened to carry the additional loads imposed by the header. This is done easily by nailing another rafter directly to the outside of each trimmer. This "sister" rafter must be cut to fit exactly between ridge and wall plate. Use a bevel square to copy angles from the existing trimmers and nail each sister securely to the trimmer rafter. Once the sister is in place, nail the cut edges of the roof sheathing to the doubled rafters.

10 **Framing the Face Wall.** The face wall of the dormer usually is framed with 2x4 lumber, 16 inches on center. Framing details are the same as those for a regular exterior wall, though you may have to improvise the stud spacing somewhat because of the small size of the wall. Consult the instructions that came with the window to determine the size of the rough opening. Assemble the wall on the attic floor and tilt it into place. Cut one end of the corner posts to match the roof pitch, then cut them to length to fit under cap plates. Nail corner posts to studs and cap plates and toe-nail them through the sheathing into the rafters.

11 **Cutting Dormer Rafters.** There are several ways to calculate the length of a rafter (you can even get books filled with precalculated rafter tables). Beginners, however, find it easiest to draw a full-size rafter layout. Measure the appropriate dimensions for the header and face wall, then use a carpenter's square and chalkline to draw a cross-section view of the header and face wall on the attic floor. Draw in the rafter and use a bevel square to copy the plumb cuts. The dormer's end rafters are doubled, and they get a different cut at the top because they land on main roof rafters instead of meeting the upper header. To find this cut, draw the roof pitch line as shown in the drawing. Remember to allow for the sheathing thickness. Then lay out the pattern on rafter stock, make your cuts and hold the rafter in place. Check for fit, and use it as a template for cutting the remaining rafters. Rafters must be 16 inches on center. The rafter tail level cut must be at least 4 inches long to allow room for soffit vents.

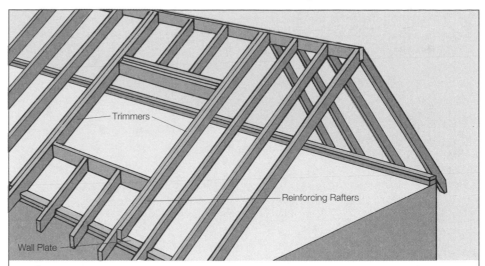

9 Cut two rafters to fit alongside the trimmers and nail them to the trimmers using 16d nails. The top of the reinforcing rafters fits against the ridge, while the bottoms rest on the wall plate.

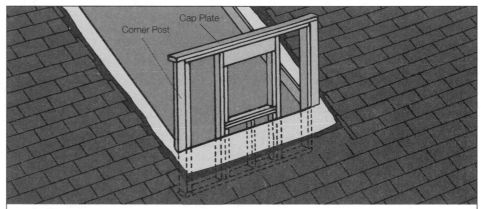

10 Assemble the face wall and tip it into place. Plumb it and nail it to the floor and trimmer rafters with 16d nails. Toenail each stud to the bearing plate. Install corner posts.

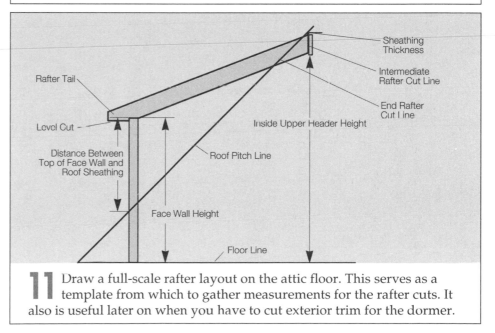

11 Draw a full-scale rafter layout on the attic floor. This serves as a template from which to gather measurements for the rafter cuts. It also is useful later on when you have to cut exterior trim for the dormer.

12 **Installing Rafters.** Lay each rafter in place and toenail it first to the header and then to the top plate—this is done without climbing onto the roof. Periodically check the face wall to make sure it remains plumb and straight.

13 **Framing the Sidewalls.** Trim away an additional 3½-inch swath of roofing on each side of the dormer to make room for 2x4 wall plates. Nail each plate through the roof sheathing and into the trimmer rafters, then lay out the locations of the sidewall "studs" so that they are 16 inches on center

(see chapter 6). Cut the sidewall studs to approximate length, then hold each one in place, mark the angle with a bevel gauge, and cut them to fit between plate and rafter. Toenail each stud in place and add blocking (if necessary) at the top of the sidewall to provide a nailing surface for sheathing.

14 **Applying Wall and Roof Sheathing.** Use exterior-grade plywood or OSB for sheathing. Apply the wall sheathing first—it stiffens the dormer and makes the installation of roof sheathing less risky. On both surfaces (but particularly on the

walls) use large pieces wherever possible. Do not use scraps. This may seem wasteful but it makes the dormer very strong.

15 **Roofing the Dormer.** After installing rake boards, fascia, edge flashing and roof felt, install the shingles just as you would on a roof. Start from the lowest edge and work your way up to where the dormer roof intersects the main roof. Pry up the first course of shingles above the intersection and slip the new shingles beneath them. You may have to adjust the exposure of each shingle course as it is installed.

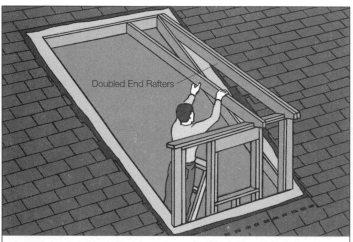

Doubled End Rafters

12 Use two 16d nails on each side of the rafter to toenail it to the header and two more to toenail it to the wall plate. Check the wall frequently for plumb.

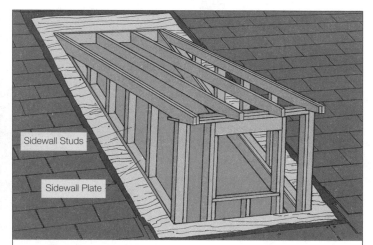

Sidewall Studs

Sidewall Plate

13 Each piece of sidewall framing is angled top and bottom to fit the plate and the doubled dormer rafter. Use a bevel square to replicate the angles. Use three 8d nails to toenail the top and bottom of each stud.

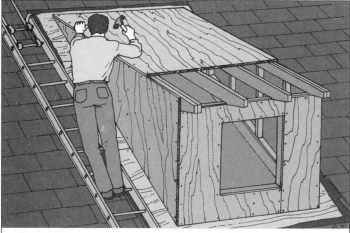

14 Seams between plywood roof and wall sheathing are 1/8 in. wide to allow for expansion and contraction. Use 6d nails to nail sheathing 6 in. on center at the edges and 12 in. on center at intermediate supports.

15 Shingles used on the dormer match those used on the rest of the house. Use four roofing nails to install them over asphalt felt underlayment. At the top of the dormer slip new shingles beneath existing shingles.

16 **Installing the Window.** This is definitely a two- or three-person job. Lift the window through the rough opening if you can; this is easier and safer than lugging it up a ladder and carrying it across the roof. Have one person hold the window flush against the sheathing while another person plumbs and levels the window from inside. Then secure it to the framing. (see chapter 4).

17 **Flashing the Walls.** The metal flashing installed around dormer walls is much like the flashing around a skylight. The metal used may be aluminum, galvanized steel, or another type of metal. Install the apron flashing first, then slip step flashing beneath each course of roof shingles. The work goes slowly when you get to the small space where the two roofs meet, but extra attention here ensures a leak-free dormer.

18 **Completing the Exterior.** You can install the siding, soffits, soffit vents, and all remaining window trim before painting the dormer. Do not forget to install a gutter; water cascading onto the roof below quickly damages shingles. Whenever possible route the downspout to another gutter. If this is not possible put an elbow at the bottom of the downspout and aim the water in the right direction to reduce its impact on the roof shingles.

Building a Gable Dormer

Even though most of its wall framing is similar to that of a shed dormer, the multiple roof planes of a gable dormer make it a more difficult project. Cutting and assembling the rafters sometimes seems complicated but at least you have the roof framing of your own house to serve as a model. The trickiest part of gable framing arises in places where the dormer meets the surrounding roof; at the valleys. The compound angles and careful detailing required at the valleys makes this a project for those who have advanced carpentry skills.

16 A flanged window is nailed directly to the sheathing. An assistant inside the dormer helps level the window as you hold it in place.

Step Flashing

Base Flashing

17 Purchase step flashing that matches the exposure of the roof. Slip each piece into place as you replace shingles alongside the dormer. The siding laps over the tops of the flashing.

18 To complete the exterior add trim, gutters and siding. Wood trim cannot rest directly on the roofing at the top of the gable. Cut it slightly short so water does not soak into the unprotected end grains of the wood.

Framing a Gable Dormer. The walls of a gable dormer can be framed like a shed dormer or the face wall can rest on a header as shown here.

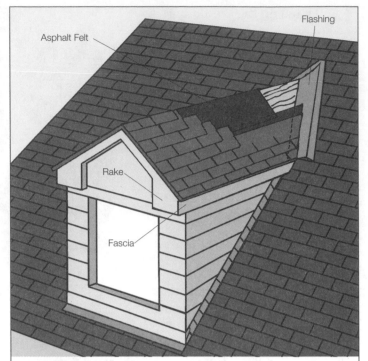

Finishing a Gable Dormer. Roofing for a gable dormer is like the main roof in miniature.

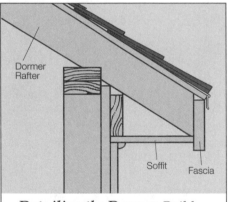

Detailing the Dormer. Build soffits and fascias for a dormer as you would for a main roof.

Framing a Gable Dormer. The walls and face wall of a gable dormer can be framed just like a shed dormer, or the face wall can rest on a header as shown. The dormer ridge projects horizontally from the main roof with rafters supporting it on each side. Note that the ceiling joists are in the same plane as the upper header.

Finishing a Gable Dormer. The dormer essentially is a miniature version of a standard roof and is shingled the same way. Particular care must be taken where the dormer intersects the main roof. Metal flashing beneath the shingles protects both valleys.

Framing Variations

The framing method described in this chapter features straightforward techniques that most amateur carpenters can handle. But it is not the only way to build a shed dormer. If you find some of the techniques unsuitable for your project or your skills use the following list as a guide to alternatives.

■ Rather than driving nails through the inside trimmer, support the header and bearing plate with metal framing anchors nailed to the side of the trimmer rafters.

■ Some people prefer a flat ceiling inside the dormer. Ceiling joists can be installed after step 13 of Building a Shed Dormer. Insulation is added between the joists rather than between the rafters.

■ Rather than cutting the rough opening from outside the attic (steps 4 and 5), work from the relative security of the attic itself. Use a reciprocating saw to slice through the roof (including shingles) and remove one bay at a time. This is messy and time consuming but may be worth the effort if the roof is steep.

■ To accommodate extra insulation use 2x6s instead of 2x4s to frame the roof.

■ In order to more evenly distribute loads to the attic floor joists some carpenters double both the bottom and top plate of the face wall.

Detailing the Dormer. Each side of a gable dormer has a soffit and can be trimmed out as shown.

Constructing Ceilings & Walls

Almost all attic conversions call for the construction of new walls and ceilings. Whether the walls are full-height partitions or half-height knee walls, framing them properly makes it much easier to install the finished wall surfaces later in the project.

1 The bottom of the ceiling joist is installed 1/2 in. above the finished ceiling. Make sure the ceiling joists are level.

2 Joists must be angled on each end to match the roof pitch. The cuts need not fit exactly, so do not spend too much time on them.

3 Snap a level chalkline across the rafters to position joists. Sight down the row of rafters to be sure they are in the same plane.

Installing Ceiling Joists

Though some people prefer the look of a vaulted ceiling in an attic conversion, a flat ceiling gives the attic a look that is more in keeping with other rooms in most homes. It is easier to install ceiling lights in a flat ceiling and by creating a mini-attic above the new room, a flat ceiling also allows for the use of gable vents. The ceiling joists are spaced 16 inches on center, and are at least 2x6 in dimension. If the joists span more than 10 feet however, use 2x8s or 2x10s.

1 **Locating the Joists.** Decide exactly how high you want the finished ceiling to be, and then add 1/2 inch (the thickness of the drywall) to determine the height of the joists. At this point, mark a horizontal layout line on a pair of opposing rafters. Measure across the opposing rafters at the level of the layout lines to determine the joist length.

2 **Cutting a Template.** Use a bevel gauge to copy the angle of the roof onto the stock; then use a circular saw to cut it. Test-fit the joist, and if it is correct, use it as a layout template for cutting the rest of the joists. Note that the fit against the underside of the roof surface need not be exact.

3 **Marking the Rafters.** Mark the height of the joists onto several additional rafters and snap a chalkline between the marks. Align the bottom of the joists to the chalkline and use two 16d nails on each end to nail the joists into the sides of the rafters. Double-check each joist for level as it is installed.

Partition Walls

A partition wall extends to the ceiling, dividing the attic space. It does not, however, play a role in the structural integrity of the house. In an attic, partition walls are used to enclose a bathroom or to divide the attic into separate rooms. Usually the walls used in an attic are not very large so they can be built one at a time on the subfloor and then tipped into place. If space is limited, however, you may have to piece the wall together in place. In addition, in the places where a partition wall meets a sloped ceiling a series of angled studs must be cut to fit between the wall plates that follow the ceiling slope.

Using the Tip-Up Method

Most partition walls are built with 2x4 lumber and most have a single top and bottom plate. If a wall contains the drain line for plumbing fixtures, however, you might want to use 2x6s to frame it. All ceiling framing or collar ties must be in place before the walls are framed. There usually is not enough room to slip them into place afterwards.

1 **Marking the Location.** Use a framing square to ensure square corners, and a chalkline to mark the exact location of the wall on the subfloor. If you are working alone drive a nail partway into the subfloor to hold one end of the chalkline as you snap it. (Or, if you have one, have a helper hold one end.)

1 Lay out the position of the walls using a framing square and a chalk line. Mark an X on the side of the line that will be covered by the plate.

2 **Laying out the Plates.** Cut two plates so that they are the same length as the wall. Align the plates and measure from one end, marking for studs at 16-inch intervals on center (the standard spacing for studs). Continue to the other end of the plates even if the last stud is less than 16 inches from the end. To check your work mark a point exactly 4 feet from the end of the plates. If done correctly the mark will be centered on one of the stud locations.

3 **Cutting the Studs.** Wall studs are cut to the height of the wall less twice the thickness of the lumber (to account for the thickness of the plates). Count the number of layout marks on the plates to get an estimate of the number of studs needed. Then cut the studs; they must be square.

4 **Building the Frame.** Separate the plates by the length of a stud and set them on edge with the layout marks facing each other. Lay all the studs in approximate position, then drive a pair of 16d nails through each plate into the ends of each stud. Use the marks to align the studs precisely.

5 **Forming a Corner.** To provide a nailing surface for the drywall, add an extra stud to each end of the wall that is part of an outside corner. One method of building the corner involves nailing spacers between two studs and then butting the end stud of the adjacent wall to this triple-width assembly. Another method is to use a stud to form the inside corner of the wall. Use whichever method you find most convenient.

6 **Raising the Wall.** Slide the bottom plate into approximate position according to the subfloor layout lines. Then lift the wall upright. With a helper to prevent the wall from toppling over, align the bottom plate with the layout lines made in step 1. When you are satisfied with the location of the wall, nail a pair of 16d nails every 2 feet or so through the bottom plate into the subfloor (into joists wherever possible). If the ceiling in the room below is made of plaster use long screws rather than nails to fasten the plate (this prevents the ceiling from cracking).

2 Use a combination square to mark the position of each stud on the plates. By marking the plates simultaneously, you can be sure the layouts match.

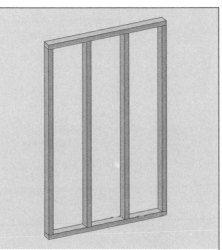

3 Use a circular saw to cut each stud to fit exactly between the plates. Stud length is the wall height minus 3 in.

4 Using 16d nails, attach the studs and plates, keeping them aligned and flush. Blunted nail tips will not split the plate.

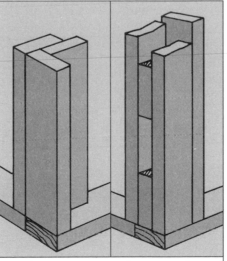

5 Corners must have a nailing surface for drywall. The left method requires less lumber; the one on the right uses up scraps.

6 When raising a wall, tip it fully upright and then slide it into position according to layout marks.

7 Use a level to plumb the wall. Check several places on the wall, as you nail the top plate.

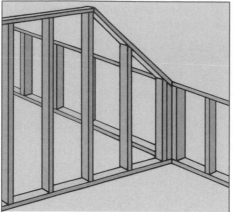

8 As you join walls, consider how the drywall will be installed. Add extra framing or blocking if necessary.

7 Plumbing the Wall. Use a carpenter's level to ensure that the wall is plumb. Adjust the frame as necessary and nail through the top plate into the ceiling framing (or into blocking if the wall is running parallel to the ceiling framing).

8 Joining Intersecting Walls. In the places that walls intersect, you will need additional studs to provide support for drywall. Add a single stud to the end of the intersecting wall and a pair of studs on the other wall.

Building a Wall in Place

When there is not enough room to assemble a complete stud wall in the confines of the attic subfloor, the wall must be built in place.

Each stud is slipped between top and bottom plates.

1 Installing the Top Plate. Cut both plates to the length of the wall and mark them for the position of the studs (studs are located 16 inches on center). Determine the location of the top of the wall and hold it up there (make sure the stud layout faces down so you can see it). Then use a 16d nail to attach the top plate to each intersecting rafter.

2 Locating the Bottom Plate. To transfer the location of the plate to the subfloor, hang a plumb bob from the top plate in several successive locations, marking them as you go. Align the bottom plate with the layout marks, adjusting it until you are sure that it is directly below the top plate. Then use pairs of 16d nails to nail it to the subfloor (keep the nails away from the stud locations already marked on the plate).

3 Installing the Studs. Measure between the plates at each stud location and cut studs to fit. Place a stud in position against the layout

1 When nailing the top plate to the ceiling joists set the nailheads flush with the surface of the plate (otherwise you may have trouble fitting studs into place). Check the plate for straightness as you work.

2 Use a plumb bob to position the plate, then nail it to the subfloor. Transfer stud locations from the top plate to the bottom plate in the same way.

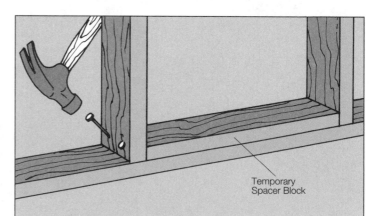

3 A stud may shift off the layout lines as it is toenailed to the plate. Hold studs in place with a temporary spacer block. Make sure the nail does not poke through the other side of the stud.

marks and use 12d nails to toenail it to each plate. Make toenailing a bit easier by using a spacer block to keep the stud from shifting. Cut the block to fit exactly between studs (if the stud spacing is 16 inches on center and the studs are 1½ inches thick, the block will be 14½ inches long). Remove the spacer as successive studs are toenailed.

Building a Sloped Wall

Some walls have one or two top plates that match the angle of the rafters. For example, if ceiling joists were installed for a flat ceiling and you want the wall to go all the way across the attic, there will be three top plates: one under the ceiling joists and one under each sloping section

of the wall. In any case, a sloping wall can be built in place much like a partition wall. The major difference is that the studs vary in length and have angled cuts at the top.

1 Installing the Plates. If the wall is situated between rafters install 2x4 blocking between the rafters to provide a nailing surface for the top plate of the wall. There always must be at least two blocks for every wall; longer walls may need blocks on 2-foot centers. If blocking is installed snap a chalkline across the blocks to mark the position of the top plate. Nail the top plate to the blocks or to the bottom of a rafter. Drop a plumb line at both ends of the top plate to mark the position of the bottom plate. Nail the bottom plate to the floor.

2 Marking Stud Locations. Lay out the stud locations 16 inches on center across the bottom plate. Then use a plumb bob to transfer these locations to the top plate. Do not try to lay out the positions by measuring along the angled top plate; if you do, the studs will not be 16 inches on center.

3 Capturing the Angle. To replicate the angle of the rafters use an adjustable bevel square placed against a level.

4 Cutting the First Stud. Measure the distance between plates to get the length of the first stud (measure to the "high" side of the angle). Then set the angle on a circular saw and cut across the face of the stud.

5 Cutting Successive Studs. Measure and cut the second stud just as you did the first. Then hold the two against each other and measure the difference in length between them. You can use this measurement, called the common difference, to determine the length of all remaining studs that are spaced the same distance apart. Each one is longer (by the amount of the common difference) than the one before it .

6 Installing the Studs. Use a pair of 10d nails at the top and three 10d or 12d nails at the bottom of each stud to toenail them into place. Use a spacer block or your foot to

1 Blocking provides a nailing surface for top plates located between rafters

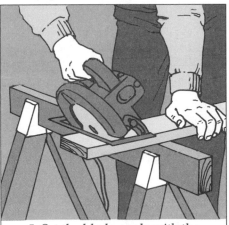

2 Use a plumb bob to transfer the stud layout on the bottom plate to the top plate.

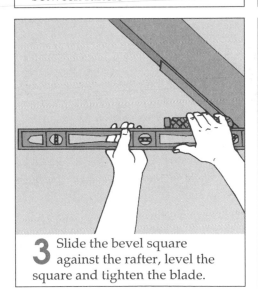

3 Slide the bevel square against the rafter, level the square and tighten the blade.

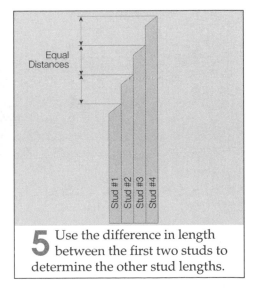

4 Set the blade angle with the bevel square. Hold the wood securely, and slowly make the cut.

Equal Distances

Stud #1 Stud #2 Stud #3 Stud #4

5 Use the difference in length between the first two studs to determine the other stud lengths.

6 Nail into the top of a stud until the nails just poke through the ends, then put the stud into position and complete the nailing.

keep the bottom of a stud from shifting as it is nailed.

Installing Doors & Door Framing

The framing around attic doors is fairly simple to build because the partitions are not load bearing and there is no need for a structural header above the door. Many do-it-yourselfers find prehung doors easiest to install (they can be installed whether or not a structural header is in place). These factory-assembled units eliminate some rather fussy carpentry work. Because the size of the rough opening depends on the size of the door and its frame, however, pur-

chase the door before you frame the wall. The rough opening generally is 1/2 inch wider and 1/4 inch taller than the outside dimensions of the jamb.

Installing Knee Walls

Knee walls are the walls that extend from the floor of an attic to the underside of the rafters. They are not very tall: 4 feet is a common height because it matches the width of a drywall sheet. The 2x4 studs typically are spaced 16 inches on center. In most cases knee walls are not structural; the rafters continue to carry the roof loads. A knee wall can be adapted easily during the framing stage to support drawers, cabinets and other objects that make use of space in the eaves. Another good idea is to build in some sort of access to the spaces behind the walls. This allows you to do routine maintenance and to install additional electrical outlets if ever the need arises.

Structural Knee Walls. If the wall has to support sagging rafters it may call for a structural knee wall. In this case the wall must be designed not only to carry the loads but to transfer them properly to a part of the house that can bear them. Plywood is glued and nailed to one or both sides of the knee wall, turning it in effect, into a

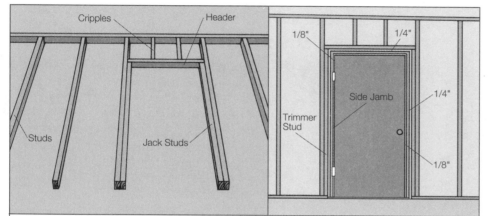

Installing Doors & Door Framing. In a wall that contains a door, be sure to account for jack studs and trimmers on the bottom plate. Clearances around the door (rough opening) are found in the manufacturer's instructions.

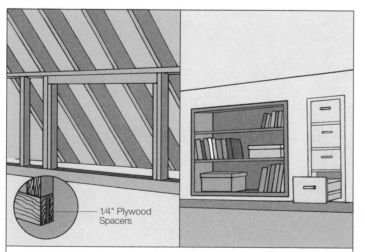

Installing Knee Walls. You can build a shelving unit in a nonstructural knee wall. The unit is a plywood case that fits into the rough opening. The drawers fit between studs.

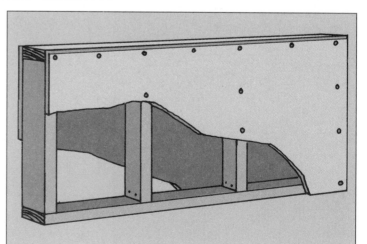

Structural Knee Walls. If a knee wall will support undersized rafters or other loads, have it designed by an engineer. By gluing and nailing plywood to the framing, a very strong beam is created.

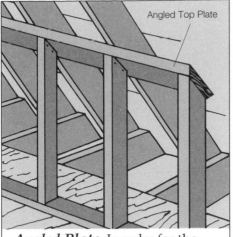

Angled Plate. In order for the front edges of studs and plates to be in the same plane the top plate must be ripped from 2x6 stock.

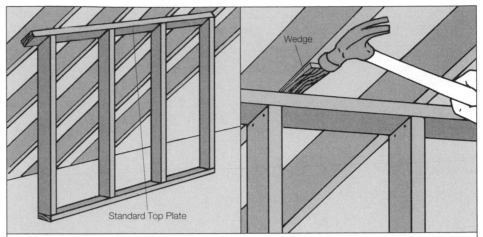

Standard Plate. A wall with a standard 2x4 top plate (left) is easier to build than one with an angled plate. Use wood wedges to fill gaps between plate and rafters. Wedges will be snug, but not so tight that they push the rafter out of position (right).

giant beam. Sometimes the bottom plate is doubled in order to distribute loads over the floor system. But because the details of structural knee walls must be worked out with care, it is best to let a structural engineer design them. The fee for such work generally is modest. Drawings and calculations that the engineer provides become a part of your permit for the job.

Building Knee Walls

A nonstructural knee wall has a single top plate and a single bottom plate. Though the stud spacing can be varied somewhat, remember that the wall has to support drywall and therefore a stud is needed for each vertical joint. There are several ways to construct knee walls.

Angled Plate. Some builders prefer to rip an angle along the edge of the top plate in order to provide plenty of support for the drywall. The angle is best cut on a table saw. Use 2x6 stock (otherwise the plate will not fully cap the studs). Assemble the wall, then tip it into place and secure it with 16d nails. To make nailing easier adjust the stud layout so that you can nail through the plate into each rafter.

Standard Plate. A knee wall that has a 2x4 top plate is easier to build than one that has an angled plate. After

assembling the wall, tip it into place. Use wood shims if necessary to make sure the wall is tight against the rafters, then nail through the plate and into the rafters with 16d nails and secure the bottom plate with 16d nails.

Drywall Nailers. Both of the methods above result in a solid knee wall that has plenty of blocking for finished wall surfaces. However, you also must provide blocking to support

the ceiling edges. The best way to do this is to cut 2x4 blocks to fit between the rafters (measure each space between rafters to account for small differences in the spacing). Attach one end of each block by face-nailing through a rafter into the block with 16d nails. The other end will be inaccessible to face-nailing so toenail it to the rafter with 8d nails.

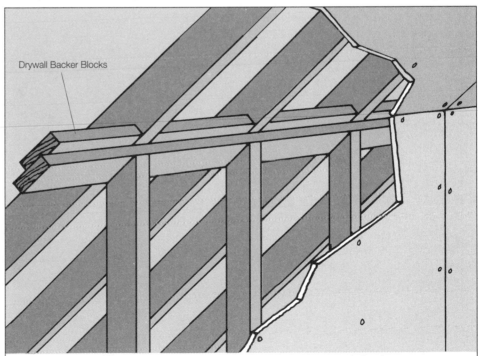

Drywall Nailers. The ceiling drywall must be supported where it meets the top of the knee wall. Use a scrap of 2x4 nailed to the rafters to "back" the drywall.

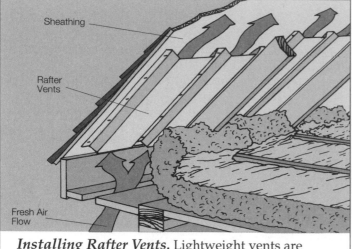

Installing Rafter Vents. Lightweight vents are stapled to the sheathing to ensure that air can pass from the soffit into the rafter bays.

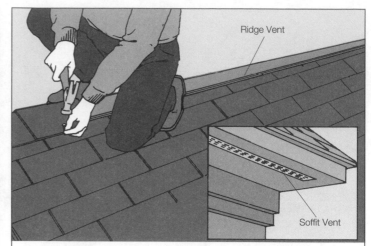

Ventilating the Roof. Ridge and soffit vents provide airflow beneath the roof sheathing. Shingles can be nailed to a ridge vent to make it unobtrusive.

Providing Ventilation

It is very important to allow at least 2 inches of clear space above ceiling insulation. This space allows the moisture that migrates through the insulation to exhaust through roof vents. In hot weather the ventilation also helps keep the underside of the roof sheathing cooler.

Installing Rafter Vents. If insulation already exists in the attic floor look for it near the wall plates. Often times the insulation found there blocks the air coming in through soffit vents. To ensure ventilation, channel rafter vents are installed in the lower portion of the rafter bays.

Ventilating the Roof

The ideal strategy for roof ventilation is to draw in air through soffit vents and exhaust it through a continuous ridge vent (a ridge vent is the only effective option for a vaulted ceiling). Other vent combinations such as gable vents and soffit vents, can be used as long as an ample amount of air flows over the insulation.

Installing Insulation

Check with local building officials to determine the amount of recommended insulation. Amounts vary considerably depending on the severity of the climate. Install insulation meticulously because gaps "short circuit" the thermal envelope and encourage drafts.

Caution: *When working with insulation be sure to protect yourself from the fibers that inevitably get released into the air. Wear a dust mask, eye protection, a long-sleeve shirt, hat, gloves, and long pants when cutting or moving insulation.*

Existing Insulation. Some insulation may already exist between the joists of what will be the attic floor. This insulation does not have to be removed as long as it does not stick up more than a few inches above the level of the joists. Insulation reduces some sound transmission through the attic floor. By leaving it in place you avoid the very messy job of removing it.

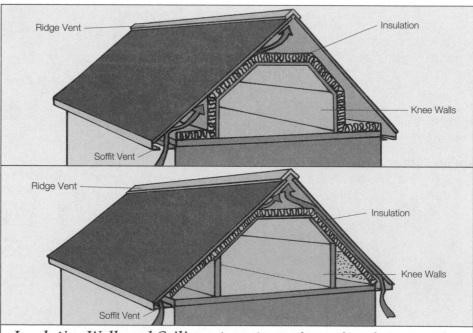

Insulating Walls and Ceilings. A continuous layer of insulation in ceilings and knee walls ensures a tight thermal envelope (top). With knee walls used for storage, insulate the rafter spaces all the way to the outside wall plate (bottom).

■ Use nails that are 1⅜ inches long to install drywall that is 1/2 inch thick. Be sure to get nails that are designed specifically for use with drywall.

■ Space nails 7 inches apart on ceilings, 8 inches apart on walls. Do not nail closer than 3/8 inch or further than 1/2 inch from the edge of a sheet.

■ The head of each nail must be set slightly below the surface of the drywall. This is called "dimpling," and allows the nailhead to be concealed with joint compound later on. A standard hammer cannot make a proper dimple because it is likely to damage the face paper. Use a special drywall hammer that has a slightly convex face instead.

■ If you make the mistake of driving a nail too hard and the face paper breaks, the nail will not hold. Drive a second nail nearby to ensure proper holding.

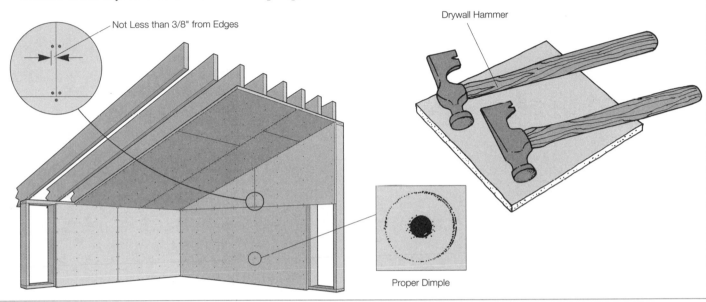

Not Less than 3/8" from Edges

Drywall Hammer

Proper Dimple

Insulating Walls and Ceilings.
Properly installed insulation keeps an attic comfortable throughout the year. Though various products can be used, fiberglass batts are the easiest to install, particularly when it comes to the sloped rafter bays of the ceiling. Some people insulate the entire roof system, running insulation all the way from ridge to eave. This often is done when knee walls contain built-in storage that would be difficult to insulate behind. Other people opt for the smallest possible thermal envelope by insulating the knee walls and just part of the ceiling.

Using Rigid Insulation.
The recommended amount of insulation is expressed as an "R" value. The higher the R value, the more effective the insulation (for example, R-38 is recommended for roofs in much of the Northeastern United States). You may find that the rafters in your attic are not deep enough to house the recommended amount of insulation. If this is the case consider installing fiberglass batt insulation with rigid insulation nailed underneath. Rigid insulation has a thermal resistance of at least R-4 per inch making it a very effective insulator that does not diminish a great deal of attic headroom.

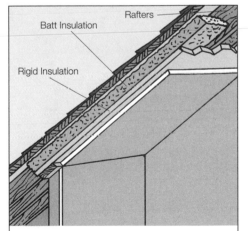

Rafters

Batt Insulation

Rigid Insulation

Using Rigid Insulation. If joist bays are too shallow for effective insulation, install what fits and nail rigid insulation to the rafters.

Finishing Walls & Ceilings

Just about any wall or ceiling surface can be used in an attic including solid-wood strip paneling, sheet paneling (plywood and others) and drywall. Drywall (also known as plasterboard, gypsum board or by the trade name Sheetrock) is the most commonly used material because it is versatile and relatively inexpensive. Some codes require that drywall be installed beneath other wall surfaces to provide a measure of fire safety.

Types of Drywall

Regular drywall has a dark gray kraft paper backing. The front is covered with smooth, off-white paper that

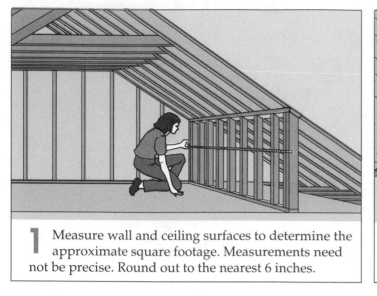

1 Measure wall and ceiling surfaces to determine the approximate square footage. Measurements need not be precise. Round out to the nearest 6 inches.

2 Score a straight line on the face of the drywall sheet and snap it along that line. Keep your fingers well away from the cutline when using a razor knife.

takes paint readily. The long edges of each 4x8-foot sheet are tapered slightly to accept tape and joint compound. Standard drywall comes in several thicknesses; a 1/2-inch thickness usually is appropriate for attic conversions. Some types of drywall have special purposes. Water-resistant drywall, usually blue or green in color, is made for use in areas of high moisture such as around bathtubs. Fire-resistant drywall, called Type X, is required by some local building codes.

Installing Drywall

1 **Estimating Your Needs.**
Calculate the square footage of the ceiling and each wall. Then add these figures to get a total for the entire room. Add 10 percent more to this figure (to account for waste) and then divide by 32 (the number of square feet in one 4x8 sheet). The result is the approximate number of drywall panels needed for the job. If the attic has a lot of complicated or odd-shaped surfaces, however, you may opt to do a more detailed estimate. If so, draw each surface to scale and then determine the number of panels needed .

2 **Cutting Drywall.** Place one sheet on a flat work surface and use a razor knife guided by a straightedge to score the face paper. Shift the drywall so the score line overhangs the work surface; then snap it along the line. Slice through the paper backing to remove the piece.

3 **Installing the Ceiling.** A 4x8 sheet of drywall is heavy and awkward to handle so you will need assistance when it comes time to install the ceilings. Cut a sheet to size, then lift it into place and hold it firmly against the rafters. Quickly nail in several locations at the center of the sheet to hold it in place. With a helper or two supporting the sheet use a chalkline to mark the position of rafters and then complete the nailing.

4 **Installing Walls.** The drywall is installed vertically on partition walls so that the tapered edges of each sheet fall over a stud. Sheets sometimes are applied horizontally

3 With at least two people, press the drywall against the ceiling joists and nail from the center of the panel towards the edges.

Using Nails or Screws

Drywall nails are the original way of attaching drywall. Many professionals still use nails because nails are cheaper than screws, and if you are experienced, nailing can be faster. Another advantage of nailing is you don't need an electric drill or screwdriver and you don't have to drag around its extension chord. Use 1⅝-inch ring-shank drywall nails for 1/2-inch drywall, and 1⅞-inch nails for 5/8-inch drywall.

A newer method is to install the drywall with drywall screws. You can drive these screws with any variable speed electric drill equipped with a hex-head bit. Or, you can buy or rent a "screw shooter." This is a high-speed electric screwdriver with an adjustable clutch. The clutch stops driving the screw when it is just below the surface of the drywall, but before it breaks through the paper surface. This creates a dimple that is much smaller and a little easier to fill with joint compound than the dimple produced by a hammer. Use galvanized screws that are at least 1 inch longer than the thickness of the drywall.

Lever

4 Whenever possible, use a lever to lift the sheets into place instead of trying to hold them up single-handedly.

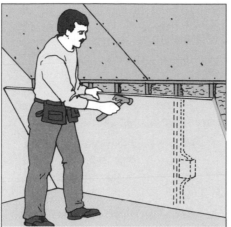

5 Stagger joints between ceiling and wall panels. Apply lipstick to an outlet; press the drywall against it to mark its location.

to minimize the number of seams between them, but this requires the installation of blocking between the studs. If you have to lift the panel slightly in order to maneuver it into position use scraps of wood to make a foot-operated lifting lever. The edge of the lower panel is butted firmly but not forcibly against the ceiling panel which already is in place.

5 **Marking for Cutouts.** Cut holes in the drywall to accommodate electrical boxes. Use lipstick to mark the outside edges of each box, then cut a sheet of drywall to the proper size and push the box firmly into position. The lipstick marks where to make the hole. Use a keyhole saw or a special drywall saw to cut it.

Finishing Drywall

After the drywall is in place the seams and nail dimples, as well as imperfections such as accidental gouges, are concealed in a multi-step process called "finishing." This work must be done meticulously because even the smallest dents and ridges show through paint and wallpaper.

Tools and Materials. A thick paste-like material called joint compound is the main ingredient for finishing drywall. Several layers of compound are spread over imperfections and

each layer is sanded smooth after it dries. Compound is available in several formulations but the "all-purpose compound" is suitable for most applications. Inexpensive paper tape (sold by the roll) is embedded in the compound to reinforce seams and prevents cracks from appearing at these locations. A 100-grit sand-paper can be used to smooth dried joint compound. However, open-weave silicon-carbide paper does not become clogged with sanding dust as standard papers do and it lasts longer. Even better yet, if you

can find it, is drywall sanding mesh which does not clog at all.

Several taping knives of different sizes are necessary to spread the compound and smooth wet seams. Each knife has a thin flexible steel blade. Though knife size is partly a matter of personal preference, a 10-inch and a 14-inch knife are good for smoothing joints, and a 4- or 5-inch broad knife is good for applying the first coat and for filling nail dimples.

Caution: *Wear goggles and a dust mask (or respirator) when sanding.*

1 **Filling Flat Joints.** Use the smallest knife to force the compound into the tapered drywall joints until they are filled and level. At butt joints (where the nontapered ends of two panels join) fill the crack and create a slight hump (this will be flattened later).

2 **Embedding the Tape.** Cut a length of joint tape and center one end of it over the joint, then embed the tape by using the smallest knife to smooth it into the compound. Spread a 1/8-inch-thick layer of compound over the tape. Hold the knife at a 45-degree angle and go back over the joint to scrape away the excess compound.

1 Use a 4 in. knife to spread joint compound over a seam. The compound fills the tapered area between two drywall sheets.

2 Cut paper tape to the length of the seam, center it over the seam and use the smallest knife to smooth it into place.

3 **Finishing inside Corners.** Start by filling both sides of the inside corner joints with compound. Fold a length of paper tape along its center-line and apply it to the joint (the tape is precreased for this purpose). Remove excess compound as in step 2. If you find the inside corners difficult to finish use an angled taping knife called an "inside corner taping tool" to help you.

4 **Finishing Outside Corners.** If there are any outside corners use tin snips to cut a length of metal corner bead to the height of the wall. Angle the cut ends inward slightly to ensure a better fit and use drywall nails to attach the bead to the wall. Using the edge of the bead to guide the knife, fill the bead with joint compound.

5 **Finishing Knee Walls.** The intersection of the knee wall and the ceiling forms an angle that is dif-

ficult to finish using standard paper tape. A solution to this problem is to use multi-flex tape instead. This simply is paper tape that is reinforced with two metal ribbons. The metal side faces the wall and stiffens the tape just enough so that it is easy to form an obtuse angle.

6 **Filling Nail Dimples.** Use the smallest knife to fill all nail dimples and other minor imperfections with compound. No tape is required.

7 **Applying Finish Coats.** After the first coat is dry inspect the seams and remove all ridges that might interfere with the smoothness of subsequent joints. Ridges can be scraped off with the 4-inch knife or lightly sanded (with experience the first coat will be so smooth that you can skip this step). Then use the 10-inch knife to apply a thin second coat of compound to the joints. Use the 4-inch knife to "spot" the dimples

again. After the second coat dries use the 14-inch knife to spread the third and final coat. Spot dimples only if they are not filled completely.

8 **Sanding the Compound.** After 24 hours, or when the compound is completely dry, sand all joints and dimples until smooth. Fold a sheet of 100-grit sandpaper into quarters and go over the compound lightly. Be careful not to sand through the face paper.

Use a "universal pole sander" to make the work easier This tool has a pad with clamps to hold sandpaper or drywall mesh. The pad is swivel-mounted to a pole. This tool particularly is handy for reaching ceilings but you may find yourself using it almost everywhere because it extends your sanding stroke. Brush or vacuum away all traces of sanding dust before painting or papering the walls.

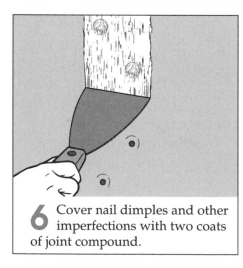

3 When working on inside corners, be careful not to cut the tape with the corner of the knife.

4 On outside corners, the knife rides along the corner bead, so make sure nails are set below it.

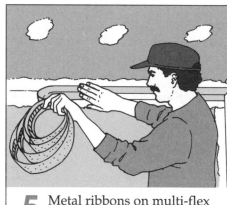

5 Metal ribbons on multi-flex tape make it easier to use on odd angles.

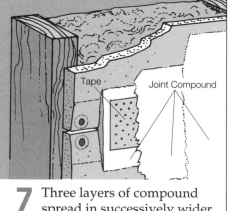

Tape

Joint Compound

6 Cover nail dimples and other imperfections with two coats of joint compound.

7 Three layers of compound spread in successively wider swaths make a finished joint.

Universal Pole Sander

8 Sand joints as necessary. Shine a bright light across the walls to check your work.

Actual dimension The exact measurements of a piece of lumber after it has been cut, surfaced, and dried. Example: A 2x4's actual dimensions are 1½x3½.

Bottom plate Also known as a sole plate; a horizontal framing member attached to the subflooring that supports the wall studs.

Building codes Municipal rules regulating safe building practices and procedures. Generally encompasses structural, electrical, plumbing, and mechanical remodeling and new construction. Confirmation of conformity to local codes by inspection may be required.

Cant strip An angled strip of wood installed at the perimeter of a skylight as extra protection against water infiltration.

Curb The wooden frame that elevates a skylight above the plane of the roof.

Dormer A window set upright in a sloping roof, and the roofed projection in which the window is set. There are a variety of styles including gable, shed, and eyebrow. Dormers afford increased headroom, natural light from windows, and increased ventilation.

Drywall Also known as wallboard, gypsum board, plasterboard, and by the trade name Sheetrock; a paper-covered sandwich of gypsum plaster used for wall and ceiling surfacing.

DWV (Drain, waste, vent system) The system of piping and fittings inside the walls used to carry away plumbing drainage and waste.

Fish tape Flexible metal strip used to draw wires and cable through walls, raceway, and conduit.

Flanged window A window that is manufactured with a perimeter nailing flange to facilitate installation.

Flashing Material used to prevent seepage of water around any intersection or projection in a roof including vent pipes, chimneys, skylights, dormers, and roof valleys.

Floor loading An expression in pounds per square foot for the maximum weight that joists are allowed to bear according to code. "Dead" loads refer to the static weight of the building materials while "live" loads vary with room occupants and furnishings. Factors effecting load limits include: joist wood species, joist thickness and depth, joist spacing, and distance between joist supports.

Gable The triangular area of exterior wall of a building.

Header A structural member that forms the top of a window, door, skylight, or other opening to provide framing support and transfer weight loads. Header thickness must equal wall width.

Joist One in a series of parallel framing members that supports a floor or ceiling load. Joists are supported by beams or bearing walls.

Knee wall A wall that extends from the floor of an attic to the underside of the rafters. Knee walls are short (usually 4 feet high) and often non-bearing.

Load-bearing wall A wall that is used to support the house structure and transfer weight to the foundation.

Nominal dimension The identifying dimensions of a piece of lumber (e.g., 2x4) which are larger than the actual dimensions (1½x3½).

On-center A point of reference for measuring. For example "16 inches on center" means 16 inches from the center of one stud to the center of the next.

Penny (abbreviated "d") Unit of nail measurement. Example: A 10d nail is 3 inches long.

Pitch Number of inches a roof rises per 12 inches of run. Example: A shallow roof would be 4 in 12 and a steeper roof would be 9 in 12.

Plumb Vertically straight, in relation to a horizontally level surface.

Rafters Dimensional lumber that supports the sloping roof of a structure.

Ridge board The horizontal framing piece to which the rafters attach at the roof ridge.

Ridge The horizontal line at which two roof planes meet when both roof planes slope down from that line.

Riser The vertical member of a stair between treads.

Sash The framework into which window glass is set. Double-hung windows have an upper and lower sash.

Service panel The point at which electricity provided by a local utility enters a house wiring system.

Sheathing The wooden covering on the exterior of walls and the roof. Typically made of 1/2-inch construction-grade plywood; older homes may have shiplap or planks.

Sistering The process of reinforcing a framing member by joining another piece of lumber alongside it.

Slope The degree of inclination of a roof plane in inches of rise per horizontal foot of run.

Stringer Diagonal boards that support stair treads, usually one on each side and one in the middle of a staircase.

Stud Vertical member of a frame wall, placed at both ends and usually every 16 inches on center. Provides structural framing and facilitates covering with drywall or paneling.

Subfloor The floor surface below a finished floor. Usually made of a sheet material such as plywood.

Toenail To fasten two pieces of wood together by driving nails at an angle through the edge of one into the other.

Top plate Horizontal framing member, usually consisting of doubled 2x4s, that forms the top of a wall. Attaches to the tops of wall studs and supports floor joists and rafters.

Tread The horizontal boards on stairs, supported by the stringers.

Trimmer stud Studs attached to full studs to support a header in window and door openings. Distance between trimmer studs is the rough opening width for doors and windows.

Trusses A roof framing system with rafters supported by crossed webs. An attic with trusses is not suitable for conversion to living space.